Endorsements

"Robby Roberson has done an excellent job depicting the life of Simon Peter as recorded in Scripture. This book is sure to enlighten, encourage, and challenge its readers as the Word of God is presented in a fresh and powerful way. Peter was certainly not a perfect disciple, but he truly loved the Lord, learned from his failures, and was used greatly to further Christ's Kingdom. May God bless you as you read his story."

—Dr. Jeff Schreve
Pastor, First Baptist Church Texarkana, Texas
From His Heart Ministries

"I have known Pastor Roberson for almost 50 years, and he has always had a sincere desire to both know the Word of God and to teach it to the people of his church. He is a humble pastor who loves God's Word. In his book, *Peter: The Man Who Went on an Adventure with Jesus*, Pastor Robby walks with Peter as he walked with the Lord, and we go along with them for the life-changing journey too. This book is a must read for pastors, bible teachers, and Christians everywhere. The exegesis and applications for each chapter is well worth the price of the book. Enjoy it (you will) and use it to help others in their walk with the Lord (you must).

—Pastor Larry V. Wood (Ret)

The challenge for every serious Bible reader is finding the nexus between antiquity and the present. In this precocious analysis of the life and thought of Simon Peter, Pastor Robby Roberson achieves this diachronic divide with the skill of a diver working the depths of another world. Do not miss finding yourself in the life of Peter!

—Dr. Paige Patterson, President
Sandy Creek Foundation

With the heart of a pastor and the skills of an advanced exegete, Robby Roberson provides us with an inspirational study of the life of Peter. This read opened my eyes even wider to the adventures of the apostle who preached at Pentecost. From success to failure and back again this fisherman is great to study, and Pastor Roberson is very successful at applying those lessons to us who are today seeking to rebound from our own bold stumbles. This is a great study, laced with opportunities for introspection and encouragements to restart and claim fresh victories. I would think it also would be a great study for groups. A chapter per week would lead to many applications and challenges that would naturally emerge from those who, like Peter, are willing to press forward to success. I have known this pastor for over two-thirds of his life. He is a gifted preacher and a shepherd who smells of sheep. That is, he walks with his flock and loves them as he leads them. Like his Lord, he lays down his life for his sheep. You will see his heart in this study and that is also what makes it a must-read.

—Dr. Tom Hatley
Senior Pastor
Immanuel Baptist Church
Global Outreach Center
Rogers, Arkansas

I recommend this commentary by Pastor Robby Roberson without reservation. For more than four decades I have shared this simple truth with people from every walk of life, "The greatest adventure in life is to know God, know God's will for your life and do it!" Robby shows the Apostle Peter found this to be true in his incredible journey with the Lord Jesus. Robby writes with a scholar's mind, the clarity of a prophet's voice, and with the tenderness of a shepherd's heart. I read the book in one day; I simply could not put it down! This is an insightful read for every Christian leader.

—Dr. Tony Crisp, PhD
True Life Concepts Ministry
Knoxville, Tennessee

My dear friend, Robby Roberson's new book is an in-depth look at the amazing life and ministry of the Apostle Peter. The author reveals the unique character of Simon Peter in both his boldness and his blunders. Robby's use of narratives beautifully illustrates Peter's humanity, and yet his potential for greatness. Quotes used from great men of God are timely, as well as riveting. It truly is a labor of love for the Lord Jesus and His Holy Word. Read this book a "day" at a time, and like me, you will be challenged intellectually, emotionally, and spiritually.

—Robert E. Grimm, DD
Pastor, First Baptist Church
Southwest City, MO

I love character studies, and Pastor Robby has given us one of the best character studies on the life of the apostle Peter that I've ever read. Both a new believer and a seasoned saint can be blessed by this book

—Dr. Phil Neighbors
Senior Copastor
Valley Baptist Church
Bakerfield, California

Peter

The Man Who Went On An Adventure With Jesus

Blessings on your adventure with Jesus!

Robby

2 Cor. 4:5-7

Justine McIlvain

Acts 2:38

Robby Roberson

ISBN 978-1-63903-514-4 (paperback)
ISBN 978-1-63903-515-1 (digital)

Christian Faith Publishing
832 Park Avenue
Meadville, PA 16335
www.christianfaithpublishing.com

Printed in the United States of America

Contents

FOREWORD

My parents reared four children. We are all fairly close in age and all, believe it or not, in Christian ministry. That ultimate "ministry" destination for each of us might make you assume we were also somewhat angelic as children. Nothing could be farther from the truth! Apart from the grace of God and His hard, sanctifying work, I shudder to think where we might be now. I am sure you can identify!

A case in point: When my siblings and I gather, someone always brings up what has become known as "Tom's Bad Day," a day when it seemed everything went wrong for me in spite of my best efforts. An errant arrow pierced two window panes. A mistaken throw of a baseball, two more! And the same baseball thrown on my bed in disgust bounced, breaking another window. An attempt to absolve my wrongdoing by washing the family car resulted in two flat tires, pierced as I drove over a broken-off fence stake. One more window was broken when, alone in our basement, I threw a knife at a board, only to see it ricochet through another window. At day's end, I could account for six broken windows and two flat tires. Oh, and the lost chamois and bent spoon only added to the misery. So now, over sixty years later, my family feels obligated to occasionally refresh my memory of a really bad day! Thanks to loving, forgiving parents, I've lived to write about that day!

Special days, memorable in their impact, punctuate each of our lives. Simon Peter, that remarkable apostle of the Lord Jesus, lived through many such days himself. It seemed that his personality—open, inquisitive, bold to the point of brashness and decisive to the point of impulsiveness—was a ready invitation to such memorable, meaningful, life-changing days.

My friend, Robby Roberson, has captured the essence of those days on the pages of the book you now hold in your hand.

You cannot miss the fact that most chapters begin with the words, "The Day!" That is why this book will be of much value to you! I don't know about you but I can readily identify with Peter! I've had such "days" and I am sure there are more ahead. I am also sure you can identify, as well. Each of those "days" has its lesson, unique to the moment and more valuable than gold. Robby Roberson gives us a front-row seat from which we can see Peter AND ourselves; and from that perspective, we can learn about God's rich, enduring love and provision for our lives.

Read this book you will discover yourself! And, best of all, you will come face-to-face with the Lord and His grace for each day! Yes, read on! That way you'll be well prepared to meet the next "day" of your life.

Tom Elliff
Pastor and Author
President Emeritus, International Mission Board, SBC

ACKNOWLEDGMENTS

I wish to say thank you to every church that has had the courage to allow me to serve in a pastoral role. Through my many shortcomings and failures and my rare successes, God's people have loved me and my family, encouraged me, blessed me, forgiven me, and taught me. After more than forty years, I truly am enriched by the people of God and love the people of God.

I especially want to thank the people of Grace Place Baptist Church. It has been my privilege to invest my life among this people for about three decades. They are truly a people of grace to me. They believed in me when I didn't believe in myself very much. They let me develop while forgiving my mistakes. They patiently let me lead when it sometimes took me an inordinate amount of time to discover where the Lord Jesus wanted to go. They have been patient, kind, and gracious. I love this people with all my heart, and I hope this book is a gift to them and their willingness to invest in me.

I also want to say thank you for all those I have served with in staff positions over the years. I have learned and benefitted from each and every one of those relationships. I count it a privilege to have served the Lord Jesus with you! Thank you too to all those who have mentored me or invested in me over the years.

I am blessed to present to you in this work the artistic talents of Justine McManus. I count Justine and her husband, Barry, as precious friends. They have served in various pastoral staff positions and as international missionaries. Their family is just exceptional, and I had the privilege of being their pastor for about four years. During that time, I became aware of Justine's unique method of taking a message and capturing it in artistic form. I asked her to capture each chapter of this book in a single drawing. I believe you are going to be absolutely blessed by her work!

Finally, but most significantly, I want to thank my family. My wife, Mellanie, has been my co-laborer for all these years. She recently told me that it had been her goal all these years to never harm *my* ministry. The truth is that it has always been *our* ministry (really Jesus's ministry), and she has faithfully served by my side through every up and down and every twist and turn. She has been an absolutely wonderful wife, mother, lover, ministry partner, Christ-follower, and friend. Her support in ministry and even in this project has encouraged me on.

Parenting came after a call to ministry for me, and I had anxieties about parenting as a pastor. I wanted my children to fall in love with Jesus, and I wanted them to love His bride, the church. Michael, Rachael, and Charity—you are amazing. I thank the Lord for who you are and for your heart for Him. I am honored to be called your dad. Thank you for your support and understanding through the years, and I am thankful for the legacy that is building in our family through the sweet grandchildren and mates you have brought our family's way.

INTRODUCTION

I have always loved biographical series. It seems to me that principles of the Word come to life through the lives of the biblical characters and therefore become easier to grasp and apply. They warn us against sin and encourage us in our walk with Him. This was especially affirmed to me years ago when I discovered these two New Testament passages:

> For whatever was written in former days was written for our instruction, that through endurance and through the encouragement of the Scriptures we might have hope. (Rom. 15:4 ESV)

> Now these things took place as examples for us, that we might not desire evil as they did. (1 Cor. 10:6 ESV)

I find the life of Peter especially intriguing. His story has some mystery. He seems to burst on the scene of the New Testament. We are uninformed regarding his birth, his childhood, or his adolescent years. We know little about his family except that he had at least one brother (Mark 1:16), he was the son of Jonah (or John, Matt. 16:17), and that he was married (Matt. 8:14).

In many ways, Peter is the *everyman* or *everywoman* of the Scripture. His humanness allows us all to relate and to see ourselves in him. We feel his victories and suffer with him in his failures.

His story is almost abrupt. We enter his life at what appears to be young adulthood as he meets Jesus and everything changes! It is quite an adventure!

An adventure can be seen as simply the sum of day-to-day experiences with Jesus. So that is what we will observe with Peter—the different day-to-day experiences in his walk with the Lord as presented to us in the Scripture. Let's enjoy it together!

1

The Day I Left Everything

Luke 5:1–11

In June of 2018, our church was kind enough to send my wife and I on a cruise and inland train excursion to Alaska. It was the trip that we never dreamed we would be privileged to take, and it was a gift to celebrate our twenty-fifth anniversary serving as lead pastor at the church.

One of the highlights of the trip for me was when a gentleman named Allen Moore stepped onto our car on the train and spent about twenty minutes telling his story.

Allen was an Arkansas native who moved to Alaska twenty-five years prior and became a world champion sled dog racer. He is a three-time winner of the Yukon Quest International Sled Dod Race, a one-thousand-mile race that takes days to complete and has temperatures that reach –60 degrees! At the time we encountered him, Allen had won the Yukon three times (2013, 2014, 2018). He also held the fastest time ever (eight days, fourteen hours, twenty-one minutes); and he was the oldest winner ever (age fifty-three).

In his story (and many others we heard while in Alaska), I was captured by the spirit of adventure in his life. It seemed to be the driving force for this radical life that faced terrible obstacles in pursuit of something big.

Allen reminds me of Simon Peter, a simple Galilean fisherman, who encountered Jesus Christ. That encounter became the driving force to an adventure with Jesus that produced a radical life that faced terrible obstacles in pursuit of proclaiming the good news of the kingdom.

Speaking of obstacles, this passage presents one. Even though it is our first look at Peter, the incident here is not his first encounter with Jesus. "Luke already had stated that Jesus had healed Simon's mother-in-law which denotes previous contact with Simon and Andrew."[1] And I agree with Warren Wiersbe that

> this event is not parallel to the one described in Matthew 4:18–22 and Mark 1:16–20. In those accounts, Peter and Andrew were busy fishing, but in this account they had fished all night and caught nothing and were washing their nets (if nets are not washed and stretched out to dry, they rot and break).[2]

Therefore, it seems likely that this was at least the third time Jesus had contact with Peter, but this is where everything changed. In fact, it caused me to dig deeply into both John and Luke's accounts, which I believe happened on different days. I was looking for evidence of conversion in John's account of a prior meeting with Jesus. As I compared them, I noted some significant differences:

- The word *follow* in John's account (*akoloutheo* = "to follow, travel") does not have the significance that it has in the Luke account. It just means they went with him and spent the day with Him.
- Clearly, Andrew gives testimony regarding Jesus. "We have found the Messiah" can mean the result of a search or to accidentally find Him. The search is definitely over because a perfect tense verb is used!
- Andrew brings Peter to Jesus, but there is no clear evidence of a conversion during this encounter. In fact, Jesus uses

the future tense in regard to Simon's coming name change (which probably is symbolic of the transformation to a new man).

- In Luke's account, the word *master* is important (5:5). It is the word *epistates.* It is used six times in Luke in place of *rabbi* (it is a Lukan word). It means chief or commander and seems higher than *didaskale* (teacher) but not as high as *kurios* (Lord), which Peter will use in verse 8! This word for *master* is used only by Luke and is a term for very high respect. Some commentators even say that it is always used of the disciples (implying that Peter is one in verse 5), but it is not so (17:13; see also 8:24, 45; 9:33, 49). Peter is using a term of great respect in verse 5, but I do not believe that he is yet a disciple.
- Luke uses both name titles (Simon, Peter) throughout the book, but this is the only time he uses them together, and I wonder if that is significant in light of what happens when he uses them.
- It is critical to me how *follow me* is used in Luke (see 5:27–28; 9:23, 57, 59, 61; 18:22, 42). It is always used in conversion language, genuine life change, full surrender.

So I believe that this *day* is when Peter is converted. I believe that this is the starting point—this day that *he left everything and followed him* (v. 11). It was the *day* that fully launched his *adventure with Jesus.*

There appear to be several things that prepared Peter for this life-changing day where he confessed his sins and left everything to follow Jesus. One thing that seems obvious is *the demonstration of God's power.* Prior to this, according to Luke, he has already experienced other demonstrations of God's power. He witnessed the healing of his mother-in-law and others with various sicknesses (4:38–44). He had at least heard of a man being freed from a demon (4:31–37). And here, he would encounter a demonstration of God's power again.

> And Simon answered, "Master, we toiled all night and took nothing! But at your word I will let down the nets."
>
> And when they had done this, they enclosed a large number of fish, and their nets were breaking.
>
> They signaled to their partners in the other boat to come and help them. And they came and filled both the boats, so that they began to sink. (Luke 5:5–7 ESV)

I agree with others who have said that if I had fished all night and caught nothing, I would probably be *selling* my nets, not washing them out to get ready to go out again! But you know fishermen; they just don't quit! Now, Jesus asked him to do something that went against his training and life experience.

> Normally, the fish that were netted in shallow water at night would migrate during the daylight hours to waters too deep to reach easily with nets, which is why Peter fished at night. Peter no doubt thought Jesus' directive made no sense, but he obeyed anyway, and was rewarded for his obedience.[3]

As a result, Peter experiences an incredible *demonstration of God's power* (vv. 6–7)!

Another thing that prepared Peter for this life-changing day is *the proclamation of the Gospel.* It appears likely that Peter had encountered that proclamation as Jesus preached around the Galilean area (Luke 4:42–44, Mark 1:14).

Finally, he is prepared for this life change by *the testimony of others.* As noted in John 1:35–42, he has been impacted by the testimony of Andrew and their partners in fishing, James and John.

These preparatory events finally culminate with an awareness of the holiness and Lordship of Jesus Christ combined with an acute realization of personal sin. Confronted with the Lord's might and majesty, he cries out in *conviction* a request that is "not to be taken literally, for where would Peter have expected Jesus to go? Rather it is idiomatic for 'Lord, be merciful to me a sinner.'"[4]

I believe that this cry led back to an *invitation* that had been previously given:

> Passing alongside the Sea of Galilee, he saw Simon and Andrew the brother of Simon casting a net into the sea, for they were fishermen.
>
> And Jesus said to them, "Follow me, and I will make you become fishers of men."
>
> And immediately they left their nets and followed him. (Mark 1:16–18 ESV)
>
> And, now, there is *surrender* to that invitation to follow Jesus and catch men. Luke notes that Peter (and his friends) *left everything and followed him*. (v. 11)

It is interesting that my own adventure with Jesus began in a similar fashion as Peter. I wasn't fishing, but over the course of about a two-year period, there were preparatory events that included hearing *the proclamation of the Gospel* in a very clear way. On at least three occasions, I heard *the testimony of others* about their life-changing encounter with Jesus. Lastly, a young evangelist came to stay in our home for a week, and I saw *the demonstration of the power of God* in and through his life in a way I had never seen before.

All those things culminated one Saturday night in December of 1975, as I returned home from a date and walked into the home of my parents. My mom asked me what was wrong and the conviction of my sin reached a breaking point. I confessed my lostness, and she led me down the "Roman road" (Romans 3:23; 6:23; 5:8; 10:9–10, 13), and I knelt in my parents' den surrendering to the Spirit's invitation to surrender wholly to the Lordship of Jesus over my life.

It was the beginning of an incredible adventure with Him! I have since observed this sequence of events in the lives of hundreds of others as they began their own adventure with the Lord Jesus.

How about you? How about an adventure that transcends the majesty of Alaska and the glory of the Yukon Quest? How about an adventure that will change your life and your eternity? How about finding Jesus worthy of giving up everything and following Him?

2

The Day I Had a Sinking Feeling

Matthew 14:22–33

Steve Callahan had loved boats and been around them all his life. By his twenties, he was designing and building them, one of which was a 6.5-meter sloop named *Napoleon Solo*. In 1981, he sailed her alone across the Atlantic, something he had dreamed of since he was twelve. On the return journey, the first week was calm, and then a gale started, but he had been through much worse. Late at night, something—probably a whale or a shark—smashed into the boat, creating a hole in the hull. He awakened with water thundering over him, knowing that she was sinking fast.

Unable to stay aboard *Napoleon Solo* as it filled with water and was overwhelmed by breaking seas, Callahan escaped into a six-person Avon inflatable life raft, measuring about six feet across. He stood off in the raft but managed to get back aboard several times to dive below and retrieve a piece of cushion, a sleeping bag, an emergency kit containing, among other things, some food, navigation charts, a short spear gun, flares, torch, solar stills for producing drinking water and a copy of *Sea Survival*, a survival manual written by Dougal Robertson, a fellow ocean survivor.

He would drift for 1,800 nautical miles across the ocean for the next seventy-six days. While adrift, he spotted nine ships that did not spot him or his flares. He was rescued by fishermen who picked him up just offshore having been drawn to him by birds hovering over the raft, which were attracted by the ecosystem that had developed around it. During the ordeal, he faced sharks, raft punctures, equipment deterioration, physical deterioration, and mental stress. By the time the fishermen reached him, he had lost a third of his body weight, and it would take six weeks before he could properly walk again.[5]

Steve Callahan definitely had a sinking feeling. So did Peter on this day at the Sea of Galilee. The story begins with an interesting word: "*Immediately* he made the disciples get into the boat and go before him to the other side, while he dismissed the crowds" (Matt. 14:22 ESV).

It is fascinating that Jesus so intentionally puts the disciples in the boat. It appears to me that there are two reasons for this. John gives the first reason to us.

> When the people saw the sign that he had done, they said, "This is indeed the Prophet who is to come into the world!"
>
> Perceiving then that they were about to come and take him by force to make him king, Jesus withdrew again to the mountain by himself. (John 6:14–15 ESV)

This is following the miracle of feeding the five thousand. Jesus wanted to disburse the crowd knowing that motives for kingship were not his motives and that they were operating out of God's will and outside of God's timing.

I believe that the second reason has to do with what had just happened. The feeding of the five thousand had been such a great victory. Immediately and intentionally, Jesus puts His men to the test. I believe Peter would say of this day that *he discovered that a great test often follows a great victory*! It is amazing how often this happens! Two classic examples are the great victory that Elijah experienced at Mt. Carmel only to immediately be tested by Jezebel and Jesus' baptism, which included empowerment of the Spirit and affirmation of the Father followed by the temptation of the devil.

Since the text says that Jesus "made the disciples get into the boat and go," I believe that Peter would also tell us that this day caused him to *discover that storms come even in the will of God.* Jesus had tested them like this before (Matt. 8:23–27). On that occasion, He had been in the boat with them. Now he would test them by being out of the boat.

We must be careful judging life based upon our circumstances. I love the words of Warren Wiersbe, "This storm came because they were *in* the will of God and not (like Jonah) out of the will of God… there are two kinds of storms: storms of *correction*, when God disciplines us, and storms of *perfection* when God helps us to grow."[6] So remember (Peter would say), you can be right in the center of the will of God and the seas of life can really get rough!

I think that Peter would also say that he *discovered that he should be encouraged because Jesus is praying.*

"And after he had dismissed the crowds, he went up on the mountain by himself to pray. When evening came, he was there alone" (Matt. 14:23 ESV).

What wonderful encouragement for the Christ-follower today! You may be on the sea and you may be in a storm, but the Lord Jesus is in heaven praying for you (Heb. 7:25)! Be encouraged to endure. Be encouraged to do His will!

Peter would also tell us that he *discovered that his response is often determined by his perspective.*

> But the boat by this time was a long way from the land, beaten by the waves, for the wind was against them.
>
> And in the fourth watch of the night he came to them, walking on the sea.
>
> But when the disciples saw him walking on the sea, they were terrified, and said, "It is a ghost!" and they cried out in fear.

> But immediately Jesus spoke to them, saying, "Take heart; it is I. Do not be afraid." (Matt. 14:24–27 ESV)

This text is rich in declaring their circumstances and their perspective. They had been beaten by the waves and the wind was against them. They were a long way from the land. The winds were too high for a sail even if they had one. The only alternative was rowing, and they had been rowing with all their might.

"He saw the disciples *straining at the oars*, because the wind was against them. About the fourth watch of the night he went out to them, walking on the lake. He was about to pass by them" (Mark 6:48 NIV).

This straining had gone on for some time. It was now "the fourth watch of the night," which was between 3:00 and 6:00 a.m. They had been battling for approximately nine hours! They were exhausted, and they were frightened. The text says that they "cried out in fear" (v. 26). They are almost out of their senses. In fact, when they see Jesus coming to them, they think He is a ghost!

When I was a young boy, we went to a lake called Canton Lake for the day with some family members. My dad was unable to get off work that day, so we went without him. We went across the lake from the boat ramp to an isolated beach area to play for the day, and as evening approached, we prepared to go back across the lake to meet my dad. As that time approached, the wind began to pick up and the lake became violently rough. We put the zip up side and back pieces of the boat cover on and waves were splashing over the boat as it lurched in the lake, and I was greatly frightened. But these were professional fishermen who had been on the sea many times, but they are frightened out of their minds! It was a horrific storm!

Mark's account uses an interesting phrase: "He was about to pass them by." At first glance, it seems almost cruel. Here are His men, terrified and exhausted, and He is just going to pass them by! But as Abraham Kuruvilla points out, it is nothing of the sort.

The verb *parerchomai*, pass by, is found in Exodus 33:22; 34:6; and 1 Kings 19:11 (LXX), where Yahweh showed himself to Moses and to Elijah, respectively; when both were in a crisis—God performed a passing by. Incidentally, both these OT characters crossed major water barriers (Moses, the Red Sea; and Elijah, the Jordan [2 Kings 2:8]). The verb thus turns out to be almost a technical term for a comforting epiphany, not, as it appears on the surface, an attempt by Jesus to avoid the boat in distress" (Abraham Kuruvilla, Mark, p. 136). It is interesting that the Greek text says that Jesus had been desiring (wishing, willing—imperfect tense) for some time to show His glory to His men!

Jesus is not callously passing them by. He is passing by in His glory to encourage His men in the midst of a great storm so that He might change their perspective and strengthen their faith! In fact, that is reinforced as the passage continues.

There is a second *immediately* in this passage. Jesus moves *immediately* to change their perspective. He moves to take their focus off of their struggle and onto Him! He gives them an imperative command: *Be encouraged* (or take courage). The Greek says that he then said, "*Ego eimi*," "I Am." It is a reminder of deity. It is the same name God gave to Moses so long before (Exodus 3:14). He is bigger than the storm. Don't be afraid!

I suspect that Peter would also say that on this day he *discovered that the very thing I fear often brings Jesus close to me*. He feared the storm, but Jesus came to him on the storm. I love the way that John MacArthur said it, "He used the trial as His footpath."[7] What encouragement! What a wonderful thing if God would use your storm and mine to bring Jesus close!

I think Peter would also say that he *discovered that faith that is grounded in the Word of God is capable of amazing things*. We now observe this amazing moment where Peter responds to Jesus' word to come to him and gets out of the boat and walks on water. "In all recorded history only two men ever walked on water, Jesus and Peter!"[8]

Lastly, it is my suspicion that Peter would tell us that on this day he *discovered good news…even in moments of failure we often get to see the hand of God.*

> But when he saw the wind, he was afraid, and beginning to sink he cried out, "Lord, save me."
>
> Jesus immediately reached out his hand and took hold of him, saying to him, "O you of little faith, why did you doubt?"
>
> And when they got into the boat, the wind ceased.
>
> And those in the boat worshiped him, saying, "Truly you are the Son of God." (Matt. 14:30–33 ESV)

Peter took his eyes off Jesus and put them back on the storm. At that moment of doubt and failure, we observe the third *immediately* of the passage. Immediately reached out His hand and caught him! This experience had given them another opportunity to realize that *there is no situation beyond Jesus's ability*. What a wonder when Jesus gets in the boat with us!

"And he got into the boat with them, and the wind ceased. And they were utterly astounded, for they did not understand about the loaves, but their hearts were hardened" (Mark 6:51–52 ESV).

In fact, look at the difference of the two storm incidents and the disciple's response. In the first, they said,

> And when he got into the boat, his disciples followed him.
>
> And behold, there arose a great storm on the sea, so that the boat was being swamped by the waves; but he was asleep.
>
> And they went and woke him, saying, "Save us, Lord; we are perishing."

> And he said to them, "Why are you afraid, O you of little faith?" Then he rose and rebuked the winds and the sea, and there was a great calm.
>
> And the men marveled, saying, "*What sort of man is this*, that even winds and sea obey him?" (Matt. 8:23–27 ESV)

In the second, their response is very different: "And those in the boat worshiped him, saying, 'Truly you are the Son of God'" (Matt. 14:33 ESV).

What was the purpose of this event? It was to grow their *faith muscle*! The development of our faith is incredibly important to our God. Surely, these two texts alone indicate as much:

> And without faith it is impossible to please him, for whoever would draw near to God must believe that he exists and that he rewards those who seek him. (Heb. 11:6 ESV)

> But whoever has doubts is condemned if he eats, because the eating is not from faith. For whatever does not proceed from faith is sin. (Rom. 14:23 ESV)

Notice how Peter himself says it much later in life:

> In this you rejoice, though now for a little while, if necessary, you have been grieved by various trials, so that the tested genuineness of your faith—more precious than gold that perishes though it is tested by fire—may be found to result in praise and glory and honor at the revelation of Jesus Christ. (1 Pet. 1:6–7 ESV)

In the church where I presently serve, there is a man who is a personal trainer and who has competed in Mr. Universe–type events.

His biceps are bigger than my legs! Granted he is a bigger man than me and obviously the Creator made him larger than I am. But an additional reason that his biceps are so much larger than mine is because they have consistently been exposed to the resistance of weight that have caused his muscles to develop dramatically.

So, my friend, the next time you feel like you are sinking, move your perspective from whatever is "blowing" through your life and back onto the Savior who loves you, has prayed for you, cares for you, and allowed this in your life. And remember, He is building your faith muscles! He wants to teach you that there is no situation beyond His ability!

3

The Day with the Dead Girl

Mark 5:21–43

As we trace Peter's biography and his adventure with Jesus, we will continually observe that Jesus was very intentional about building Peter's *faith muscle*. We saw it in the last chapter, and we will see it in this one. It is a good reminder to us that Jesus desires to do that with *anyone* who follows Him. The reason is because of the critical importance of faith in our lives. These two New Testament passages make that clear:

> And without faith it is impossible to please him, for whoever would draw near to God must believe that he exists and that he rewards those who seek him. (Heb. 11:6 ESV)

> But whoever has doubts is condemned if he eats, because the eating is not from faith. For whatever does not proceed from faith is sin. (Rom. 14:23 ESV)

This day of adventure comes on the heal of the incident with the Gerasene demoniac (Mark 5:1–20), which ends with the townspeople pleading with Jesus to leave but across the lake is "a large crowd" welcoming his presence. Included in that crowd were two people who were very anxious to see Him—one had lost her health; the other had lost a child. Their stories become intertwined.

The man's name is Jairus. He was one of the synagogue rulers. It is interesting that he is named for us because "except for the disciples, he is one of the few characters in this Gospel who is given a name."[9]

His circumstances remind us that there are a number of things that you and I can love and have them die. We can have a relationship with someone and have it (or them) die. We can have a profession that we love and have that profession die. We can have a dream that we love only to see that dream die. But for this man, it may have been the most difficult thing of all to love and lose—a child! Somewhere I ran across words credited to Dwight Eisenhower that put it well: "Most women say there is no greater pain than to bear a child. I say there is no greater pain than to bury one. There's no tragedy in life like the death of a child. Things *never* get back to the way they were."[10]

I have observed this personally my entire life. When I was about one year old, my parents had a little girl. They named her Neva. She was born with severe spina bifida and only lived three months. Almost fifty years later, my mom blurted out her name one day in my office and wept with grief over the loss of that child!

Now, Peter comes face-to-face with a man losing his child. In desperation, he falls at the feet of Jesus pleading for the life of his child. As he did, I believe that Peter learned more regarding *faith*. The first lesson I believe that he learned is that *faith begins with a premise.*

> And when Jesus had crossed again in the boat to the other side, a great crowd gathered about him, and he was beside the sea.
>
> Then came one of the rulers of the synagogue, Jairus by name, and seeing him, he fell at his feet and implored him earnestly, saying, "My little daughter is at the point of death. Come and lay your hands on her, so that she may be made well and live."

> And he went with him. And a great crowd followed him and thronged about him. (Mark 5:21–24 ESV)

This man was "one of the most important and most respected men in the community."[11] It couldn't have been easy for him to come in such a public way to Jesus and to plead for his help with such humility. But he was desperate. And he had a *premise.* I don't know the origin of the *premise.* I wonder if (where) Jairus had encountered Jesus before. I wonder if he was at the synagogue of Mark 3 and saw a man's shriveled hand restored. Or I wonder if he was at the synagogue at Capernaum when a demon was cast out. I simply don't know. But I do know that somewhere along the way in his life he came to a place where he believed that Jesus could and possibly would heal his daughter. It is the premise that *God is able!*

Both Jairus and the woman with the disease believe that Jesus is able to and that contact with Him will change their situations. They both had a *prior* faith that He was able. These two stories remind us of "the visible tangible fruits of faith."[12] Faith *acts*! Faith shows *persistence* in overcoming obstacles.

Please do not misunderstand. I am not encouraging faith *in faith.* If God always intervened, we would never have to exercise faith. If God always intervened, there would be no such thing as a miracle. I am simply noting that both the woman and Jairus acted believing that Jesus was able. Jairus's faith must have been greatly encouraged because *Jesus went with him* (v. 24)!

I believe that the second lesson Peter learned on that day was that *faith rests in God's timetable* (vv. 25–35a).

In the midst of getting Jesus to his dying daughter, the encounter with the woman occurs. I can only imagine Jairus's emotions. They must have gone from great encouragement to incredible frustration caused by the crowd and the delay. I can only imagine him thinking, *I was in line first. Take care of my problem first.* Do you ever become impatient while waiting in line? What if it was your daughter dying?

But maybe the wait is good. In the midst of waiting, he is going to witness someone else in need. He is going to observe her trembling in fear but telling her whole story and publicly expressing her faith. He is going to hear Jesus say to her, "Daughter, your faith has healed you. Go in peace and be freed from your suffering." And he needs to hear it all because while Jesus is still speaking the worst possible news comes.

Now, Peter learns the third lesson from this event. I believe he learns that *faith hopes when hope seems gone.*

> While he was still speaking, there came from the ruler's house some who said, "Your daughter is dead. Why trouble the Teacher any further?"
>
> But overhearing what they said, Jesus said to the ruler of the synagogue, "Do not fear, only believe." (Mark 5:35–36 ESV)

Jairus must have been crushed, and Peter saw that. Those who came with the message certainly had no hope. Some have even suggested that they sarcastically urged him to move on suggesting that "Jesus is only a teacher, and death marks the limit of whatever power he may have."[13]

Clearly, Jesus overheard their message and accepted the fact that the girl indeed was dead. The hopeless situation doesn't seem hopeless to Him. In fact, He says something interesting to Jairus, "Don't be afraid; just believe." In the Greek text these are two rapid-fire commands: "Stop being afraid" (present passive imperative) and "only believe or trust" (present active imperative).

It is the second command that captures my attention. In the face of the death of his child, Jesus commands the man to "keep on believing." It reveals that he had been trusting before and now Jesus is urging him to have hope even though hope seems gone!

When they arrive at the home, his faith is again challenged by the commotion caused by professional mourners already assembled and practicing their trade, once again confirming that there was not the slightest hope that the girl was still alive.

Finally, it must have been such a hurdle for his faith when Jesus calls the girl's death sleep because of how temporary He will render it only to be confronted with a forceful response from those gathered here. They *laughed* at Him. The word here is strong. It is "to laugh at, to ridicule." The word is only used three times in the New Testament and only concerning this occasion (see also Luke 8:53, Matthew 9:24). It should be noted that if you choose to be someone who lives by faith, don't be surprised if you are ridiculed for it! Unbelief not only laughs at God's Word; it also laughs at the follower of God who dares to trust Him! It should also be noted that "their skepticism puts them outside. There will be no miracles for the scornful throng."[14]

I wish to convey one more truth that I believe Peter learned on this *day with the dead girl*. I believe that he learned that *faith positions us to experience the miraculous*!

> And he allowed no one to follow him except Peter and James and John the brother of James. (Mark 5:37 ESV)

> And they laughed at him. But he put them all outside and took the child's father and mother and those who were with him and went in where the child was. (Mark 5:40 ESV)

The girl not only came back to life but was also healed of her sickness. It is interesting that the law required only two or three witnesses for confirmation of truth (see Deuteronomy 17:6, 19:15), but for this miracle, there are *five* witnesses!

They alone experienced the miraculous. It instructs us to stay close to Jesus. Typically, those close to Him are the ones who get to experience the miraculous! The language of verse 42 is delightful. Mark's favorite word *straightway* is used. These five were straightway amazed (astonish, to displace, to stand aside from) in great amazement (distraction, confusion, terror) when, at Jesus's command, the girl stood up and walked around! They were almost disoriented with amazement (you may have experienced moments like this where you don't know what to say—whether to laugh or cry, whether to run or fall on your face). If you want to experience more of those moments, *stay close to the Lord!*

The end of the story is also intriguing. Jesus *greatly charged* those in the room to "not let anyone know about this" (v. 43). How could you not let anyone know about this when that girl walked out of that house? I suspect that Jesus is simply asking the parents and the daughter not to reveal intimate details of the resurrection and allow He and his disciples to quietly slip away, avoiding the acclaim that would surely have followed. Still yet, can you imagine the moment that girl and her parents walked out of that home, and she was alive?!

One last thing, we must remember that someday that girl faced the experience of death again. This resurrection was only temporary. There was still an eternity to face. I think that if I arrived on the scene years later and was asked to preach the funeral of the daughter who had again died I would encourage hope once again with this passage of Scripture:

> Jesus said to her, "I am the resurrection and the life. He who believes in me will live, even though he dies." (John 11:25 NIV)

Hallelujah! The One who defeated death has promised an eternal resurrection and life after death to all who believe in Him!

The Day I Got It Right

Matthew 16:13–20

Two of the most stunning accounts of *wisdom* occur in the Bible. One is in the Old Testament and the other is in the New Testament.

The Old Testament example is in 1 Kings 3:16–28 and is the story of two prostitutes coming to King Solomon with the classic "she said, she said" story. In a dilemma where it was impossible to tell who was telling the truth and who was lying, Solomon wisely chooses the path to the truth when he ordered that the living child be cut in half, exposing the heart of the true mother and causing all Israel to hold "the king in awe because they saw that he had wisdom from God to administer justice."

The New Testament example is in Matthew 22:15–22 and is the account where the Pharisees "went out and laid plans to trap Jesus in his words." They begin with flattery and then ask Him about whether it was right to pay taxes to Caesar or not. Jesus asks to be shown a coin and then asked whose portrait and inscription was on it. When they replied "Caesar's," He then said, "Give to Caesar what is Caesar's, and to God what is God's." The text says that "when they heard this, they were amazed" (v. 22).

There is such a need for wisdom in our lives and world and many would argue that there is presently a great void of wisdom.

"We have grasped the mystery of the atom and rejected the Sermon on the Mount…the world has achieved brilliance without wisdom, power without conscience. Ours is a world of nuclear giants and ethical infants."[15]

But isn't it amazing when moments of *wisdom* come? In Peter's case, they didn't come often before the resurrection, so they really deserve to be appreciated! According to Matthew 16, there was *a day when he got it right* and wisdom spilled out of him.

> "But what about you?" he asked. "Who do you say I am?"
>
> Simon Peter answered, "You are the Christ, the Son of the living God." (Matt. 16:15–16 NIV)

Christ is the Greek equivalent of the Hebrew *Messiah*, God's predicted and long-awaited deliverer. According to Craig Blomberg, "Here is the first time in Matthew that anyone in Jesus' audiences has unambiguously acknowledged him as the 'Christ.'"[16]

This wonderful moment urges us toward several truths about *when wisdom comes.*

When wisdom comes, *it should be celebrated.*

> Jesus replied, "Blessed are you, Simon son of Jonah." (Matt. 16:17a NIV)

> "Those who truly confess that Jesus is God, which is to confess Him as Lord and Savior (1 John 4:14–15), are divinely and eternally blessed. They are 'blessed'…with every spiritual blessing in the heavenly places in Christ (Eph. 1:3–5)."[17]

This kind of wisdom should be celebrated!

When wisdom comes, *it should be received with humility.*

"For this was not revealed to you by man, but by my Father in heaven" (Matt. 16:17b NIV).

Peter did not arrive at his great confession on his own. "Man's human capabilities, here represented by the metonym *flesh and blood*, cannot bring understanding of the things of God (cf. 1 Cor. 2:14). The *Father* Himself must reveal them and bring understanding of His Son to human minds."[18] So even when wisdom comes, it should be received with humility. This is a product of divine revelation.

When wisdom comes, *it can become the springboard of opportunity* for your life and for investment in others.

> And I tell you that you are Peter, and on this rock I will build my church, and the gates of Hades will not overcome it.
>
> I will give you the keys of the kingdom of heaven; whatever you bind on earth will be bound in heaven, and whatever you loose on earth will be loosed in heaven. (Matt. 16:18–19 NIV)

This passage has been greatly debated throughout the history of the church. The issue surrounds the word play found in the Greek text. *Peter* is from *petros* meaning "small stone." *Rock* is from *petra* referring to "a massive rock." The question is, what is this massive rock?

It seems to me that there are four primary options that have emerged. The first is that "this rock" is Peter. The church of Jesus Christ will be built on Peter. The primary proponent of this view is the Roman Catholic Church. Regarding this view, I must agree with John MacArthur who said, "Such an interpretation, however, is presumptuous and unbiblical, because the rest of the New Testament makes abundantly clear that Christ alone is the foundation and only head of His church."[19]

A second view is that "this rock" refers to Jesus Himself. W. A. Criswell would be an example of those holding this view. "Peter is addressed, but Jesus indicates, possibly by means of gesture, that the Christ is the *petra* upon which the church will be built (cf. 1 Cor. 3:11)."[20]

The third view is that "this rock" is Peter's confession of Christ as the Messiah. This view has been prominent especially since the days of the Protestant Reformation and, to some extent, are a reaction to the traditional Roman Catholic position.

A final view regarding "this rock" is that it represents the apostles. An example of this position would be John MacArthur Jr. who says that

> it therefore seems that in the present passage Jesus addressed Peter as representative of the twelve. In light of that interpretation, the use of the two different forms of the Greek for *rock* would be explained by the masculine *petros* being used of Peter as an individual man and *petra* being used of him as the representative of the larger group. It was not on the apostles themselves, much less on Peter as an individual, that Christ built His church, but on the apostles as His uniquely appointed, endowed, and inspired teachers of the gospel.[21]

There seems to me to be value in all but the first view, which is clearly unbiblical. Maybe it is best to let two other New Testament passages speak:

> For no one can lay a foundation other than that which is laid, which is Jesus Christ. (1 Cor. 3:11 ESV)

> So then you are no longer strangers and aliens, but you are fellow citizens with the saints and members of the household of God, built on the foundation of the apostles and prophets, Christ Jesus himself being the cornerstone. (Eph. 2:19–20 ESV)

Regardless how you take "this rock," it is clear that Peter's moment of wisdom would indeed become a *springboard of opportunity* because he would be given "keys." "A 'key' was a sign of authority, for a trusted steward kept the keys to his master's possessions and dispensed them accordingly."[22] What Peter would bind and loose would be based upon decisions already made in heaven. Two perfect passive participles are used indicating that the text should be rendered, "having been bound and having been loosed."

This imagery of the "keys" suggests that they will close and open, lock and unlock, or that it is referring to "'Christians' making entrance to God's kingdom available or unavailable to people through their witness, preaching, and ministry."[23] We will see illustrations of Peter's privileged opportunities throughout Acts 1–12.

Finally, we must note that although this was a glorious day when Peter *got it right*, this day's wisdom was *not necessarily an indicator of continual success*. It is fascinating how this account is preceded and followed by less than wonderful moments of Peter *not* getting it right.

> But Peter said to him, "Explain the parable to us."
>
> And he said, "Are you also still without understanding? (Matt. 15:15–16 ESV)

> And when they came to the crowd, a man came up to him and, kneeling before him, said, "Lord, have mercy on my son, for he has seizures and he suffers terribly. For often he falls into the fire, and often into the water.
>
> And I brought him to your disciples, and they could not heal him."
>
> And Jesus answered, "O faithless and twisted generation, how long am I to be with you? How long am I to bear with you? Bring him here to me."

> And Jesus rebuked the demon, and it came out of him, and the boy was healed instantly.
>
> Then the disciples came to Jesus privately and said, "Why could we not cast it out?"
>
> He said to them, "Because of your little faith. For truly, I say to you, if you have faith like a grain of mustard seed, you will say to this mountain, 'Move from here to there,' and it will move, and nothing will be impossible for you."
>
> As they were gathering in Galilee, Jesus said to them, "The Son of Man is about to be delivered into the hands of men, and they will kill him, and he will be raised on the third day." And they were greatly distressed. (Matt. 17:14–23 ESV)

In the first example, Jesus calls Peter dull! In the second example, he calls him faithless! It is just a simple reminder that getting it right once doesn't mean that you will the next time.

Oh, that we might have wisdom that our Savior might celebrate! I don't know about you, but this story causes me to desire to gain wisdom. Maybe it does for you too. So let me ask the question: how can we gain wisdom? There are at least four ways encouraged in God's Word:

1. Wisdom comes through the Scripture.

   "And how from childhood you have been acquainted with the sacred writings, *which are able to make you wise* for salvation through faith in Christ Jesus" (2 Tim. 3:15–16 ESV).

   All Scripture is breathed out by God and profitable for teaching, for reproof, for correction, and for training in righteousness.

   You will never be wise apart from an intake of the Scripture! I have heard the excuse many times and have made it myself—"I don't have time." But here is the truth: we make time for what is important to us. If you truly desire wisdom, you will make time for an intake of the Scripture!

2. Wisdom comes through observation of the person of Christ.

> And because of him you are in Christ Jesus, who became to us wisdom from God, righteousness and sanctification and redemption. (1 Cor. 1:30 ESV)

> That their hearts may be encouraged, being knit together in love, to reach all the riches of full assurance of understanding and the knowledge of God's mystery, which is Christ, *in whom* are hidden all the treasures of wisdom and knowledge. (Col. 2:2–3 ESV)

Don't just look at the story of Jesus. Look at the person of Christ! Look at how He responds to life. Look at how He deals with people and situations. Look at His emotions and His reactions. You will be looking at wisdom personified!

3. Wisdom comes through community.

"Iron sharpens iron, and one man sharpens another" (Prov. 27:17 ESV).

Did you know that you were built for community? Why, the Godhead is a triune community. You were built in the image of God. You were built for community. The Body of Christ is incredibly important! You and I desperately need others in the Body, speaking into our lives in such a way that our lives are sharpened for the glory of God! I cannot express the extent of my gratefulness for how others in the Body have spoken wisdom into my life over the years that have been lifechanging for me!

4. Wisdom comes through prayer.

"If any of you lacks wisdom, *let him ask God*, who gives generously to all without reproach, and it will be given him" (James 1:5 ESV).

Who knows, dear friend, how God may choose to give you wisdom and then use it for the benefit of others! It has happened a number of times in the history of our country. One of the most amazing times, from my perspective, occurred one hundred and fifty-six years ago.

It happened in a place called Gettysburg, Pennsylvania, on a battleground there in those rolling hills. During the first days of July 1863, fifty-one thousand were killed, wounded, or missing in what would prove the decisive Union victory of the Civil War. It was a terrible, blood-filled, gruesome time. One nurse in her journal said that it was so bad that over one seven-day period, blood never stopped flowing from one soldier to the next on her table. It was so bad that pastors barely had time to breath between reading the Twenty-third Psalm over one dying soldier to the next.

Charles Swindoll describes it all well in a little piece called *Two Memorable Moments.*

> The aftermath of any battlefield is always grim, but this was one of the worst. A national cemetery was proposed. A consecration service was planned. The date was set: November 19. The commission invited none other than the silver-tongued Edward Everett to deliver the dedication speech. Known for his cultured words, patriotic fervor, and public appeal, the orator, a former congressman and governor of Massachusetts, was a natural for the historic occasion. Predictably, he accepted.
>
> In October, President Lincoln announced his intentions to attend the ceremonies. This startled the commissioners, who had not expected Mr. Lincoln to leave the Capitol in wartime. Now, how could he not be asked to speak? They were nervous, realizing how much better an orator Everett was than Lincoln. Out of courtesy,

they wrote the President on November 2, asking him to deliver 'a few appropriate remarks.' Certainly, Lincoln knew the invitation was an after-thought, but it mattered little. When the battle of Gettysburg had begun, he had dropped to his knees and pleaded with God not to let the nation perish. He felt his prayer had been answered. His sole interest was to sum up what he passionately felt about his beloved country.

With such little time for preparation before the day of dedication, Lincoln worried over his words. He confided to a friend that his talk was not going smoothly. Finally, he forced himself to be satisfied with his 'ill-prepared speech.' He arrived at Gettysburg the day before the ceremonies in time to attend a large dinner that evening. With Edward Everett across the room, surrounded by numerous admirers, the President must have felt all the more uneasy. He excused himself from the after-dinner activities to return to his room and work a bit more on his remarks.

At midnight a telegram arrived from his wife: 'The doctor has just left. We hope dear Taddie is slightly better.' Their ten-year-old son Tad had become seriously ill the day before. Since the President and this wife had already lost two of their four children, Mrs. Lincoln had insisted that he not leave. But he had felt he must. With a troubled heart, he extinguished the lights in his room and struggled with sleep.

About nine o'clock the next morning, Lincoln copied his address onto two small pages and tucked them into his coat pocket...put on his stovepipe hat, tugged whited gloves over his hands, and joined the procession of dignitaries. He could hardly bear the sight as they passed the blood-soaked fields where scraps of men's lives littered the area...a dented canteen, a torn picture of a child, a boot, a broken rifle. Mr. Lincoln was seized by grief. Tears ran down into his beard.

Shortly after the chaplain of the Senate gave the invocation, Everett was introduced. At sixty-nine, the grand old gentleman was slightly afraid he might forget his long, memorized speech, but once he got into it, everything flowed. His words rang smoothly across the field like silver bells. He knew his craft. Voice fluctuation. Tone. Dramatic gestures. Eloquent pauses. Lincoln stared in fascination. Finally, one hour and fifty-seven minutes later, the orator took his seat as the crowd roared its enthusiastic approval.

At two o'clock in the afternoon, Lincoln was introduced. As he stood to his feet, he turned nervously to Secretary Seward and muttered, 'They won't like it.' Slipping on his steel spectacles, he held the two pages in his right hand and grabbed his lapel with his left. He never moved his feet or made any gesture with his hands. His voice, high-pitched, almost squeaky, carried over the crowd like a brass bugle. He was serious and sad at the beginning...but a few sentences into the speech, his face and voice came alive. As he spoke, 'The world will little note nor long remember...,' he almost broke, but then he caught himself and was strong and clear. People listened on tiptoe.

Suddenly, he was finished.

No more than two minutes after he had begun, he stopped. His talk had been so prayer-like it seemed almost inappropriate to applaud. As Lincoln sank into his settee, John Young of the *Philadelphia Press* whispered, 'Is that all?' The President answered, 'Yes, that's all.'

> Over one hundred and fifty-six years have passed since that historic event. Can anyone recall *one line* from Everett's two-hour Gettysburg address? Depth, remember, not length, is important. Lincoln's two minutes have become among the most memorable two minutes in the history of our nation.[24]

The reason is because this giant of a man had been given wisdom from the Living God for not only this moment in history, but to impact a nation moving forward. On a day that Lincoln thought he got it wrong, he got it very, very right and God used that wisdom to shape a nation and to bring glory to Himself through Abraham Lincoln![25]

As we close this chapter, read again those wonderful words of wisdom and marvel at the amazing moments when wisdom comes, whether it is from the lips of Jesus, Solomon, Abraham Lincoln, or our guy Peter.

The Day I Saw the Glory of God

Luke 9:28–36
(See also Matthew 17:1–13, Mark 9:2–13)

"Now Peter and those who were with him were heavy with sleep, but when they became fully awake they saw his glory and the two men who stood with him" (Luke 9:32 ESV).

The *glory of God*...not many have gotten to see it. Some of the more intriguing instances to me are the following:

- Moses (Exodus 33:12–23; 34:1–7, 29–35)
- Stephen (Acts 7:55)
- The disciples (John 1:14)

In this last reference, it is likely that John is referring to this encounter in Luke 9 that included Peter, the subject of our study. Peter, James, and John were the only three who were privileged to see *the glory of God* on that day.

This event was the result of a *commitment* that Jesus had made previously. We see it in verse 28.

"Now about eight days after these sayings he took with him Peter and John and James and went up on the mountain to pray" (Luke 9:28 ESV).

After these sayings is pointing back to a promise that Jesus had made in verse 27. The promise was that *some who are standing here will not taste death before they see the kingdom of God*! This promise occurs in all three of the synoptic gospels just prior to the Transfiguration and Jesus's commitment to it is found in the phrase, *but I tell you truly,* which is "a solemn statement appearing only in the gospels and always spoken by Jesus. It introduces topics of utmost significance."[26]

And *eight days* later, that promise/commitment was fulfilled for Peter, James, and John! While it is clear that both Matthew and Mark say six days, it is not necessarily in disagreement with Luke. A simple explanation is that Luke includes the day of Jesus' confession (one day) and the day of the transfiguration (one day) and that Matthew and Mark only count the intervening days (six days).

On this day, they saw an incredible *change*. I love how Peter described it later in life:

"For we did not follow cleverly devised myths when we made known to you the power and coming of our Lord Jesus Christ, but we were eyewitnesses of his majesty" (2 Pet. 1:16 ESV).

Notice how Luke describes it:

"And as he was praying, the appearance of his face was altered, and his clothing became dazzling white" (Luke 9:29 ESV).

Altered here is translated "transfigured" by the KJV and "changed" by the NIV. The word is "a translation of the Greek term *metemorphothe*, which literally means 'to change the pattern.'"[27] Right in front of them Jesus has a dramatic change of appearance. "The word *transfigured* describes a change on the outside that comes from the inside. It is the opposite of 'masquerade,' which is an outward change that does not come from within. Jesus allowed His glory to radiate through His whole being, and the mountaintop became a holy of holies."[28] "The Greek text actually says, 'intensely white, as no fuller (launderer, bleacher) on earth could bleach them. Only Mark recorded this statement…the brightness recalls the shekinah glory of God in the Old Testament."[29]

This is a foretaste of Jesus' second coming glory (see Revelation 19:11–16). I like the way that James Brooks states it: "The transfiguration is a preview of the full establishment of the kingdom of God at the glorious return of Jesus prophesied in Mark 8:38…the transfiguration serves as a preview of the full establishment of the kingdom of God at Jesus' return."[30] This is, therefore, a glimpse of a coming event. It is a preview. It is like the previews before a movie, i.e., the coming attractions.

As this all transpired, there was a *conversation* going on. It was a conversation between Jesus, Moses, and Elijah.

"And behold, two men were talking with him, Moses and Elijah, who appeared in glory and spoke of his departure, which he was about to accomplish at Jerusalem" (Luke 9:30–31 ESV).

It appears to me that Moses is here because he represents the Law and that Elijah is representing the prophets. Jesus is the fulfillment of both the law and the prophets.

I also think that they represent both classes of believers affected by the return of Christ. Moses died and was buried (Deut. 34:5–6) and, therefore, represents those who have died in Jesus and who will be resurrected and glorified at Christ's coming in glory. Elijah was translated, not passing through the experience of death (2 Kings 2:11). He represents those who are alive at the return of Christ and are caught up in the air to be with Christ (1 Thess. 4:13–17).

We are told the content of their conversation. Only Luke mentions the subject matter of their conversation. It concerned *his departure*. The Greek term is *exodon*. So they spoke of His exodus "establishing a comparison between Jesus and Moses as leaders guiding God's people into the Promised Land."[31] The NKJV says that they spoke of his "decease." The cross looms just ahead. Moses and Elijah are here to encourage Jesus. I love the way that William Barclay says it, "when these two great figures met with Jesus, it meant that the greatest of the lawgivers and the greatest of the prophets said to him, 'Go on.'"[32]

It was as this conversation was drawing to a close that Peter made a *comment* that was apparently misguided and uninformed.

"And as the men were parting from him, Peter said to Jesus, 'Master, it is good that we are here. Let us make three tents, one for you and one for Moses and one for Elijah'—not knowing what he said" (Luke 9:33 ESV).

I can only imagine what Peter was experiencing! It was indeed a mountain top experience and he truly didn't want it to end. And

I certainly can't blame him. But what he was suggesting was indeed misguided. He implies an equality between Moses and Elijah and Jesus. And while Moses and Elijah have just encouraged Jesus to "go on" to the cross that redemption might be purchased, Peter was encouraging Jesus to stay on the mountain!

This was now met with a *command* from above that occurred right in the midst of Peter's comments. A cloud came that would have immediately reminded these Jewish men of the Shekinah glory cloud of the Old Testament. It would have immediately said that God was present. A voice is heard. It is the voice of the Father. The Father says, "This is my Son, my Chosen One." What is implied in this language is, "This One, and this One *alone*, is my Son." It happens right in the midst of Peter's language of equality. It completely refutes him!

"As he was saying these things, a cloud came and overshadowed them, and they were afraid as they entered the cloud" (Luke 9:34–35 ESV).

And a voice came out of the cloud, saying, "This is my Son, my Chosen One; listen to him!"

> A voice came from the cloud with the single command of the passage: *Listen to Him!* "Peter had erred in placing Moses and Elijah on the same level as Christ. Christ was the very one to whom Elijah and Moses had pointed. The voice of the Father interrupted while Peter 'was still speaking' (Matthew 17:5). The words were the same as those spoken from heaven at Christ's baptism (Matthew 3:17).[33]

I disagree with MacArthur's last line. The words were *not* the same! They were similar. But clearly, the Father is refuting Peter's unknowing words and commands that Peter and the others listen to a voice greater than Moses and greater than Elijah. They are commanded to listen to His Son, the Lord Jesus Christ!

The appearance of the cloud, the voice, and the content of the message were too much for the disciples. It all said that the Holy God of the universe was present, and they *fell on their faces* in terror. I want to turn here to Matthew's account.

"When the disciples heard this, they fell on their faces and were terrified. But Jesus came and touched them, saying, 'Rise, and have no fear'" (Matt. 17:6–7 ESV).

It is at this moment that Jesus touches them and *comforts* them with the words "rise and have no fear."

> What a day it was when Peter saw the glory of God! This event would mark the rest of the lives of these three men. I love how David Garland points out the parallels and contrasts between this event and the cross:
>
> - The glory revealed on the mountain is a private epiphany, while the suffering on the cross is a public spectacle.
> - Jesus is surrounded on the mountain by two prophets of old, Moses and Elijah, on Golgotha, by two thieves.
> - On the mountain, Jesus' garments glisten in his glory, on Golgotha, they take his garments from him, compounding his humiliation.
> - Three male disciples view his glory at close range; at the cross, three female disciples view his suffering from afar.
> - A divine voice from the cloud announces that Jesus is the Son of God; at the cross, one of his executioners, a Roman centurion, acclaims him to be the Son of God after his death.[34]

There are so many applicable truths for us to take away from this day in Peter's life. It is a great reminder that *God's promises are sure*. Jesus made a promise about what some of His men would see and that is exactly what happened.

The second thing I would say is that *we need to be careful with our words*. Peter had spoken not knowing what he was saying. Sometimes we need to just be quiet until we have thought through what we should say, and how, and when we should say it. In fact, it is interesting that this text ends by saying, "they kept silent." Mark's account says that "Jesus gave them orders not to tell anyone." Can you imagine?! It must have been incredibly difficult to not tell everyone! They couldn't even tell the other nine! There is certainly a lesson here about being careful and timely with our words and to only use them under the permission of Jesus.

It is also a great reminder that *even the greatest of saints fall short of Jesus*. He alone is the Messiah. He alone deserves our adoration and worship. Moses was a great man, but he was not the Messiah. Elijah was a great man, but he was not the Messiah. There are a lot of great men and women, but they all have clay feet. There is only one Jesus!

This event confronts us with the truth that *we can't stay on the mountain and follow Jesus. We must go into the valley with Him for the sake of redemption*. "How wonderful it would be to stay on the mountaintop and bask in His glory! But discipleship means denying self, taking up a cross, and following Him; and you cannot do that and selfishly stay on the mount of glory. There are needs to be met in the valley below."[35]

This passage also presses us that *we too, are to be transformed*! "Jesus experienced physical transformation in this passage. We are to experience 'moral transformation'"[36] Because we are a new creation in Christ, we are being changed into His image from one degree of glory to another, which will mean a change of character, ethics, motives, priorities, and devotion among other things. There is to be a radical change and a lost and dying world is watching to see if it happens!

> Therefore, if anyone is in Christ, he is a new creation. The old has passed away; behold, the new has come. (2 Cor. 5:17 ESV)

> Do not be conformed to this world, but be transformed by the renewal of your mind, that by

> testing you may discern what is the will of God, what is good and acceptable and perfect. (Rom. 12:2 ESV)

> And we all, with unveiled face, beholding the glory of the Lord, are being transformed into the same image from one degree of glory to another. For this comes from the Lord who is the Spirit. (2 Cor. 3:18 ESV)

What does that look like? I think that John's words give us by far the finest definition. Remember them: "And the Word became flesh and dwelt among us, and we have seen his glory, glory as of the only Son from the Father, full of grace and truth" (John 1:14 ESV).

Isn't that last phrase interesting, "full of grace and truth"? Jesus, in the display of His glory was full of grace and truth. As we are being transformed into His image, we will be full of grace and truth!

Located in the White Mountains of New Hampshire is a famous pass known as Franconia Notch. High on one of its rocky walls protrudes a granite formation that resembles the profile of an old man peering intently over the valley. It's called "the Old Man of the Mountain." Nathaniel Hawthorne drew his inspiration for *The Legend of the Great Stone Face* from that unusual rock formation.

Perhaps you remember the story. A boy by the name of Ernest lives in the valley from which he views daily a face fashioned in the mountain. His mother tells him that someday a venerable man who bears that image will visit the valley. Years go by. Great men from all walks of life come, but not one has the resemblance. Ernest reaches old age, disappointed that he had not seen his mother's prediction fulfilled. Finally, a poet of renown visits the area and listens to Ernest deliver a discourse to his neighbors. He notices in his face the visage of the great stone face on the mountain. Having gazed on that figure daily for many years, Ernest, now a venerable old man, has gradually come to bear its image.

In a sense, we take on the characteristics of the things on which we concentrate. That's why our whole being should be turned toward our blessed Lord and Savior. As His glory shines on us and into us, we will be changed into His likeness. Then others looking at us will see the marvelous transformation of Christ in us. All who are born of God should develop a likeness to Him.

And finally, because this event is only a preview, it compels us to say, "*Oh, what awaits us!*"

I have had the privilege of seeing some amazing things in my life. Depending on your list—I have seen two of the seven wonders of the world (the Great Pyramids, Petra). I have seen the beauty of places like Maui; Glazier Bay, Alaska; and Denali, Alaska—the highest mountain in North America at 20,310 feet. And I have seen the wonder of Jerusalem and the Holy Land. But it absolutely doesn't compare to what is ahead for me and every Christ-follower! Jesus prayed for me to see it! And I believe that when Jesus prays, the Father answers!

"Father, I desire that they also, whom you have given me, may be with me where I am, *to see my glory* that you have given me because you loved me before the foundation of the world" (John 17:24 ESV).

Oh, what awaits us!

6

The Day I Learned the Drachma Lesson

Matthew 17:24–27

People and money are really interesting. One of the most amazing stories I have ever heard or read regarding money came from Charles Swindoll. He said it was

> an actual situation I heard about on the radio some years ago. A woman in West Palm Beach, Florida, died alone at the age of 71. The coroner's report was tragic: 'Cause of death: *Malnutrition*.'
>
> The dear old lady wasted away to 50 pounds. Investigators who found her said the place where she lived was a veritable pigpen, the biggest mess you can imagine. One seasoned inspector declared he'd never seen a residence in greater disarray.
>
> The woman had begged for food at her neighbors' back doors and gotten what clothes she had from the Salvation Army. From all outward appearances, she was a penniless recluse, a pitiful and forgotten widow. But such was not the case.

> Amid the jumble of her unclean, disheveled belongings, two keys were found, which led the officials to safe deposit boxes at two different local banks. What they found was absolutely unbelievable.
>
> The first contained over 100 AT&T stock certificates, plus hundreds of other valuable certificates, bonds, and solid financial securities… not to mention a stack of cash amounting to nearly $200,000. The second box had no certificates, only more currency—lots of it—$600,000 to be exact. Adding the net worth of both boxes, they found that the woman had in her possession well over A MILLION DOLLARS. Charles Osgood, reporting on CBS radio, announced that the estate would probably fall into the hands of a distant niece and nephew, neither of whom dreamed she had a thin dime to her name. She was, however, a millionaire who died a stark victim of starvation in a humble hovel many miles away.[37]

In this next episode of Peter's life, we encounter a difficult passage that only appears in Matthew and is a miracle using money (some say the only miracle using money). We are certainly not surprised that Matthew, *the tax collector*, was interested in this miracle!

The story begins with a *confrontation.*

> When they came to Capernaum, the collectors of the two-drachma tax went up to Peter and said, "Does your teacher not pay the tax?"
>
> He said, "Yes." (Matt. 17:24–25a ESV)

This tax was not tribute for Rome, but it was a government-approved tax. It was a temple tax assessed on all Israelites, allowed to the Jewish religious leaders, for the operation and upkeep of the temple.

It was imposed on all Israelite males over the age of twenty and paid annually. The price of two drachma was the equivalent of about two days' wages.

Both Peter and Jesus had not yet paid their tax for that year and therefore, the collectors sought them out and Peter is brought to the forefront. He assures the collectors that his master was a taxpayer.

> And when he came into the house, Jesus spoke to him first, saying, "What do you think, Simon? From whom do kings of the earth take toll or tax? From their sons or from others?"
>
> And when he said, "From others," Jesus said to him, "Then the sons are free." (Matt. 17:25b–26 ESV)

As he enters the house, Jesus initiates a conversation with Peter regarding the subject. Jesus uses a short parable-like story to ask the *question* of whether or not He and His followers should have to pay the tax. His point is that He as King should be free of the tax and so should they who were sons of the kingdom. I like the way that John MacArthur said it,

> If there was any tax that Jesus was not obligated to pay it would have been the Temple tax. He was the One whom the Temple was built to honor and to whom its sacrifices and offerings were made. He was Lord of all the earth but supremely Lord of the Temple. Jesus called the Temple His 'Father's house' (Luke 2:49, John 2:16) and declared Himself to be greater than the Temple (Matt. 12:6). He had every right to refuse paying the Temple tax.[38]

Therefore, it is a bit startling that, having made His point, Jesus offers an incredible *consideration*.

"However, not to give offense to them, go to the sea and cast a hook and take the first fish that comes up, and when you open its mouth you will find a shekel. Take that and give it to them for me and for yourself" (Matt. 17:27 ESV).

Jesus is more concerned about offense than He is about whether or not He should have to pay. The word Jesus uses here for *offense* is *skandaliadzo*, which means "to shock through word or action, give offense to, anger, or shock" (BAGD).

To avoid unnecessary offense, Jesus directs Peter to go fish and that the first fish he catches will miraculously have a coin in it that is the equivalent of four drachmas, which would pay the tax for two people.

He teaches Peter *the drachma lesson*! I know what you are thinking, but the drachma lesson is *not*: *whenever I need to pay my taxes—go fishing!* No, the drachma lesson is this: *Christ followers must be* extremely *careful regarding offense.*

And that, for Peter as well as us, is troubling. It is especially troubling when one considers what Jesus will say in the very next chapter:

> "Woe to the world because of offenses! For offenses must come, but woe to that man by whom the offense comes!" (Matt. 18:7 NKJV).

The word for "offenses" is *skandalon*, which is the root word for *skandaliadzo*. Notice that Jesus says that they are unavoidable! The Christ-follower must be extremely careful regarding offense, but because of the human condition, it is inevitable that you and I will offend! In fact, in some cases, we *must* offend! So we must be extremely careful to not *unnecessarily* cause offense.

This leads to four important statements of application for my life and yours. The first is that *the truth can be offensive*. A good example of this is just a few chapters back in Matthew's Gospel (15:1–20). Jesus is asked by the Pharisees why His disciples break the tradition of the elders and He asks them why they break the command of God to honor their father and mother. Notice how pointed His words become:

> You hypocrites! Well did Isaiah prophesy of you, when he said: "This people honors me with their lips, but their heart is far from me; in vain do they worship me, teaching as doctrines the commandments of men." (Matt. 15:7–9 ESV)

It causes the disciples to approach Jesus with a question.

"Then the disciples came and said to him, 'Do you know that the Pharisees were offended when they heard this saying?'" (Matt. 15:12 ESV).

There is our word again: *skandaliadzo*. From the disciples' vantage point Jesus had scandalized the Pharisees with His words. But the sinless One in both thought and deed had simply told the truth. This was the true condition of the Pharisees. Sometimes the truth can be offensive (another example of this is found in John 6:53–71 and the word used in verse 61 is the same, *skandaliadzo*).

The second thing we do well to remember is that *the Gospel can be offensive*. This truth appears with some frequency in the New Testament.

"But we preach Christ crucified, a stumbling block to Jews and folly to Gentiles" (1 Cor. 1:23 ESV).

The word used here for *stumbling block* is *skandaliadzo*.

"As it is written, 'Behold, I am laying in Zion a stone of stumbling, and a rock of offense; and whoever believes in him will not be put to shame'" (Rom. 9:33 ESV).

This rock of *offense* is the root word for *skandaliadzo*, which is *skandalon*.

> So the honor is for you who believe, but for those who do not believe, "The stone that the builders rejected has become the cornerstone,"
>
> and "A stone of stumbling, and a rock of offense." They stumble because they disobey the

> word, as they were destined to do. (1 Pet. 2:7–8 ESV)

This is again the word *skandalon.*

"And blessed is the one who is not offended by me" (Luke 7:23 ESV).

This is *skandaliadzo.* Over and over we are told that *the Gospel can be offensive.* Clearly, we should not be offensive in our presentation of it, but it is often offensive to the lost because it points out sin, lostness, a need for repentance, and a single way to God.

The third word of application becomes very personal. Though the truth can be offensive, and the Gospel can be offensive, *we should not be offensive.* Our word for scandal surfaces again in these two pleas from the apostle Paul:

"Do not, for the sake of food, destroy the work of God. Everything is indeed clean, but it is wrong for anyone to make another stumble by what he eats" (Rom. 14:20–21 ESV).

It is good not to eat meat or drink wine or do anything that causes your brother to stumble.

"I appeal to you, brothers, to watch out for those who cause divisions and create obstacles contrary to the doctrine that you have been taught; avoid them" (Rom. 16:17 ESV).

The ancient wisdom writer instructed us concerning why this is so important.

"A brother offended is more unyielding than a strong city, and quarreling is like the bars of a castle" (Prov. 18:19 ESV).

And the apostle Paul plead for this to the church at Ephesus.

This description of offense uses very strong language. Whenever we are unnecessarily offensive, we can cause that offended brother to be like a strong city. An ancient world city was often built on an elevated area so that it might be a strong city, able to defend itself.

I had a real reminder of this in 2016 when my wife and I went to Israel again. On that trip we encountered the elevated city called Masada (980 feet high; the tallest building in my city is the Devon Tower, which is 844 feet high). For some (unknown) reason, my wife wanted to walk up Masada rather than take the tram. I have no idea why she wanted to do that, but I felt compelled to go with her because I was concerned that she would have some physical issues, and I would need to *carry* her. And that is indeed what happened! I almost had to carry her. She began to have some difficulty breathing and some tightness in her chest. What is funny is that we now know that she had zero blockage in her arteries, and I had over 95 percent blockage in two arteries. I had a heart episode two months later that culminated with two stints—and I am attempting to aid this woman up Masada! I want you to know it is indeed one high hill (especially with a woman on your back!).

So to use this language is to say that once you cause this kind of offense, it is tough to take it back! It is tough to get that relationship back! So beware and be careful about what you choose is worthy of offense! This is a great time to remember these words:

> I therefore, a prisoner for the Lord, urge you to walk in a manner worthy of the calling to which you have been called, with all humility and gentleness, with patience, bearing with one another in love, eager to maintain the unity of the Spirit in the bond of peace. (Eph. 4:1–3 ESV)

That leads to a final observation—*we must leave a compelling testimony*. The drachma lesson urges us to cause no unnecessary offense because we desire to leave a compelling testimony. Paul put it this way regarding his ministry:

"We put no obstacle in anyone's way, so that no fault may be found with our ministry" (2 Cor. 6:3 ESV).

The word "obstacle" is the word *proskope* and means "an occasion for taking offense."

And he urges the church at Corinth regarding this as well.

> So, whether you eat or drink, or whatever you do, do all to the glory of God.
>
> Give no offense to Jews or to Greeks or to the church of God, just as I try to please everyone

> in everything I do, not seeking my own advantage, but that of many, that they may be saved.
>
> Be imitators of me, as I am of Christ. (1 Cor. 10:31–11:1 ESV)

Please note that the chapter and verse identifiers are not inspired. 1 Corinthians 11:1 is often quoted. But the context of Paul's admonition to imitate him as he imitated Jesus is about not being offensive!

To the words of Jesus and the apostle Paul are the added words of Peter himself as an older man.

> But in your hearts honor Christ the Lord as holy, always being prepared to make a defense to anyone who asks you for a reason for the hope that is in you; yet do it with gentleness and respect, having a good conscience, so that, when you are slandered, those who revile your good behavior in Christ may be put to shame.
>
> For it is better to suffer for doing good, if that should be God's will, than for doing evil. (1 Pet. 3:15–17 ESV)

The *drachma lesson* is too frequently violated among the followers of Jesus and when it is, there is a stench rather than the fragrance of grace. There was a blatant example of it from a church pulpit in my very own state in 2013. It was recorded by someone in church and became a YouTube video for all the world to see.

The rant that became viral exposed pastor Jim Standridge of Skiatook, Oklahoma, dressing down people from the pulpit of Immanuel Baptist Church with offensive comments including telling one man, "You're not worth fifteen cents."

It is a disgusting display. It is a disgrace to grace. It is a clear violation to the *drachma lesson* that Peter learned on a day long ago.

I would like to contrast that with an incident in my dad's life a few years prior to his passing. His truck was down, and he took it to the Ford place. They told him multiple times that it was fixed, but when he would pick it up, it was clearly not repaired. Each time the bill continued to go up which was daunting to my dad and his very fixed income. They kept it over six weeks. I kept urging him to just go get it, and I would haul it to someone we could trust.

Most of my life, he had been very aggressive in how he dealt with someone or a situation like this. As I pressed him, he finally said, "I just haven't wanted to go in there. I fear that I might lose my cool and say something I don't want to say." I wanted to cheer my eighty-year-old dad because, at eighty, he was growing and finishing well, and he cared deeply about not unnecessarily offending.

May God help us to learn the lesson of the drachma, so that our testimony might be compelling instead of repulsive! Who will you be? Is there someone that you have offended, and it is now time for you to scale Masada in an attempt to reconcile with them?

7

The Day I Learned about Forgiveness

Matthew 18:21–35

I hope that in your life you have heard or seen some great stories of forgiveness. There are three that come to mind quickly that have impacted my life. The first I read very early in my Christian life. It was the true story of a young pastoral intern who forgave a group of thugs who beat him up on the streets of Chicago years ago.

The second is the story of Cynthia Swindoll. She sought forgiveness from her mother-in-law just three days before her unexpected death in what would be Cynthia's last opportunity to see her alive (I think this story is Insight for Living's most requested broadcast).

The third happened in the church I pastor. A few years ago, we invited a local newscaster to be the guest speaker at our Marriage Banquet hosted around the time of Valentine's Day. She told the incredible (and true) story of expressing forgiveness to the woman who had an affair with her first husband and helped ruin that marriage. It, like the first two, was a powerful story of grace and forgiveness.

In this episode of Peter's adventure with Jesus, he *learned about forgiveness*. It was an incredibly important lesson for him and for us because, according to Jesus, the human equation guarantees that *offenses must come!*

"Woe to the world because of offenses! For offenses must come, but woe to that man by whom the offense comes!" (Matt. 18:7 NKJV).

After hearing Jesus' instruction about what to do regarding a brother who sins against you (Matthew 18:15–17), Peter approaches Jesus and asks how *often* he must forgive him.

> Then Peter came up and said to him, "Lord, how often will my brother sin against me, and I forgive him? As many as seven times?"
>
> Jesus said to him, "I do not say to you seven times, but seventy-seven times. (Matt. 18:21–22 ESV)

I'm sure that you have heard regarding this text—Peter thought he was being magnanimous! "The rabbis, citing several verses from Amos (1:3, 6, 9, 11, 13), taught that since God forgave Israel's enemies only 3 times, it was presumptuous and unnecessary to forgive anyone more than 3 times."[39] Peter was doubling that number and adding one!

But Jesus' response far transcends Peter's seven times. The ESV renders this "seventy-seven times." A number of other translations have it as "seventy times seven" or 490 times. Whether one takes it as seventy-seven times or 490 times, the point is the same. He is saying that *the spirit of forgiveness* in His followers is to be unlimited. And then He drove home His point by way of a story.

"Therefore the kingdom of heaven may be compared to a king who wished to settle accounts with his servants" (Matt. 18:23 ESV).

The story is about the forgiveness of a king of a servant who had an unpayable debt. The text says, "He could not pay." The king stands for God. The servants, for God's people. The settling of accounts is a metaphor for judgment. And "often obedient and disobedient servants provide a contrast between righteous and wicked behavior."[40]

This story magnifies the greatness of God's forgiveness and points us to *the source of forgiveness*. As the king begins his settlement, he deals with a man with an unpayable debt. The *talent* was "the highest known denomination of currency in the ancient Roman Empire, and ten thousand was the highest number for which the Greek language had a particular word (*myrias*; cf. our *myriad*)."[41] John MacArthur has put this in historical context for us.

> From historical documents of the time it has been determined that the total annual revenue collected by the Roman government from Idumea, Judea, Samaria, and Galilee was about 900 talents. Based on those figures, *ten thousand talents* amounted to more than eleven years of taxes from those four provinces.[42]

And Craig Blomberg says that *ten thousand talents* "would have been an enormous debt, on the borderline of what the ancient mindset could have conceived. Estimates in modern currency range from several million to one trillion dollars."[43] I think that Jesus is trying to say that this debt is incalculable!

Jesus' point is unmistakable—this debt is unpayable! But the king is kind and compassionate and responds to the servant with grace and forgives the debt!

One would think that the enormity of the gift of forgiveness this servant received would have caused him to overflow with forgiveness to others. But he went out and encountered one of his servants who owed a small debt (especially in comparison to the enormity of the debt he had been forgiven). When this servant pleads exactly as he had pled, he refused and had the man imprisoned until the debt was paid.

When told of this the king called him to task. He called him a *wicked* servant and committed him to the *jailer who tortures* (literal translation of the word that is only used here in the New Testament). It is interesting that this jailer is not an executioner but a torturer. The servant is given over to severe discipline and is confined there *until he pays all he owed*! Remember that this is a debt he could not pay! This is a lifetime sentence! Warren Wiersbe has said it well. This is the worst prison. It is "the prison of an unforgiving heart."[44] Jesus' story ends with these almost haunting words: "So also my heavenly Father will do to every one of you, if you do not forgive your brother from your heart" (Matt. 18:35 ESV).

The *source of our forgiveness* is the greatness of what we have been forgiven. For the Christian not to forgive is an offense to the grace and forgiveness of God and to the Christ who has taken up residence inside them through the person of the Holy Spirit.

> Be kind to one another, tenderhearted, forgiving one another, as God in Christ forgave you. (Eph. 4:32 ESV)

> Bearing with one another and, if one has a complaint against another, forgiving each other; as the Lord has forgiven you, so you also must forgive. (Col. 3:13 ESV)

Two other things need to be said before we leave this chapter. The first is that the New Testament strongly warns us about becoming bitter.

> Strive for peace with everyone, and for the holiness without which no one will see the Lord.
>
> See to it that no one fails to obtain the grace of God; that no "root of bitterness" springs up and causes trouble, and by it many become defiled. (Heb. 12:14–15 ESV)

When bitterness is allowed to grow in the fertile soil of unforgiveness, the end result is defilement. I like the way an anonymous saint of long ago said it:

> Revenge, indeed, seems often sweet to men; but, oh, it is only sugared poison, only sweetened gall, and its aftertaste is bitter as hell. Forgiving, enduring love alone is sweet and blissful; it

> enjoys peace and the consciousness of God's favor. By forgiving, it gives away and annihilates the injury. It treats the injurer as if he had not injured, and therefore feels no more the smart and sting that he had inflicted. Forgiveness is a shield from which all the fiery darts of the wicked one harmless rebound. Forgiveness brings heaven to earth, and heaven's peace into the sinful heart. Forgiveness is the image of God, the forgiving Father, and an advancement of Christ's kingdom in the world.[45]

Forgiveness is an antidote or *serum* to bitterness. I know that this may be obvious and the language I am using is a little strange. So let me put it this way. I have an issue with snakes. I think it is because, as a child, my dad told me about something that happened to him. As a kid, he was in a hay loft and stuck his hand in between a couple of bales of hay. Unbeknownst to him, there was a den of snakes in between those bales. I don't know if my memory is accurate, but I think my dad said he was bitten thirteen times before he could remove his hand! That story always bothered me! Therefore, for me, the only good snake is a dead snake!

My concerns were heightened again a few years ago. A friend of mine, who is "tough as a boot," went out at dusky dark to turn off a water hydrant on his property. He was in flip flops on this warm summer evening and did not realize that the moisture had attracted a large copperhead. As he stepped in the copperhead's business, he was bitten.

He told me that it took them awhile to discover that only one hospital in our city has an antivenom. It then took them a bit of time to get to that hospital. It then took them time to get the doctor to administer it to him. He gave me a vivid description of how sick the poison made him and how thankful he was for the serum!

Unforgiveness is a poison that can make us incredibly sick. Forgiveness is the serum. It must come from the heart and since it is a supernatural work, it must be produced by the indwelling and empowerment of the Holy Spirit. Oh, friend, cry out to the Lord for the serum!

Finally, there must be a word about the *speed of forgiveness.* Earlier in this very gospel we are told that Jesus called for forgiveness to be sought quickly. It was to be sought so earnestly and quickly that one should even leave worship to attend to it immediately!

"So if you are offering your gift at the altar and there remember that your brother has something against you, leave your gift there before the altar and go. First be reconciled to your brother, and then come and offer your gift" (Matt. 5:23–25a ESV).

Come to terms quickly with your accuser…

While working on this story last fall, my wife and I attended a conference designed to refresh pastors and their wives. One evening during the conference there was an assigned date night. I took my wife out to eat and then to a movie. The movie we saw that night was *Unbroken: Path to Redemption.* The movie begins and ends with Olympic cross-country runner/World War II veteran Louis Zamperini standing before a barracks full of Japanese soldiers. In between those two scenes is his remarkable story.

While serving as a bombardier for the United States Army Air Forces in the Pacific, his plane crashed into the ocean because of mechanical difficulties during a search and rescue mission. There were eleven men on the plane. Eight died in the crash, three survived at sea, using two life rafts to do so (one of those would die at sea on day 33). After drifting at sea for forty-six to forty-seven days (island spotted on the forty-sixth and arrived on the forty-seventh), he landed on the Japanese occupied Marshall Islands and was captured. He was taken to a prison camp in Japan where he was brutally tortured. He was put into four different prisons while experiencing escalating amounts of torture.

His fiercest torture was at the final camp where he would spend two years. His torturer there was called "The Bird." During that period of time, he was considered one of the five worst war criminals of all time—not a good list to be on!

The "Bird" beat him mercilessly. He held him under water until he passed out. It was awful!

Following the war, he married within a year. He struggled greatly to overcome his ordeal. When he went to sleep at night, he would see the Bird again and would relive the torture in his nightmares. He began to drink. His marriage began to fail. His life was unraveling.

His wife was invited by friends to the Billy Graham Los Angeles Crusade. She attended and that night she gave her life to Jesus Christ as her Lord and Savior! She begged her husband to attend the crusade. When her invitation was joined by an invitation from some Christian friends, he relented and attended.

He attended with all his frustration, and hatred, and bitterness (and maybe a bit of alcohol). During Billy Graham's message, he got up to walk out and the Spirit of God used something Graham said at that moment to arrest his heart. The Spirit of God reminded him of something he had completely forgotten. During those days afloat at sea, he had looked up into the stars of the night and promised God that if He rescued him, he would trust Him and serve Him for the rest of his life.

That night, he trusted Christ as his Lord and Savior. His alcohol went away. His bitterness went away. His marriage was restored. He later became a Christian Evangelist with a passion for forgiveness.[46]

That is what makes those opening and closing scenes so powerful! The film ends with him going to each Japanese soldier and expressing forgiveness for the unthinkable! It was all because of the grace and kindness of the One who had so greatly forgiven him!

He spent years looking for "The Bird." He finally found him one day in a prison for war criminals. He requested a meeting, but the Bird declined. So Louis wrote him a letter saying that what the Bird had done was deplorable, but that he was able to forgive him because of the forgiveness of Jesus for his own unpayable debt! No one knows if the Bird ever opened the letter! Oh, what amazing forgiveness!

The life of a young pastoral intern calls us to forgiveness. The wife of a famous pastor calls us to forgiveness. The life of a well-known news anchor calls us to forgiveness. The life of a prisoner of war calls us to forgiveness. Most importantly, Jesus, through this powerful story calls us to forgiveness!

The day I learned about forgiveness.

70×7

8

The Day I Heard about the Benefit Plan

Matthew 19:23–30
(See also Mark 10:27–31, Luke 18:18–30)

It must be inherent in humanity that we will often make great sacrifices or take great risks if we perceive that the reward is worth it. It happens in education. There is a diploma or degree at the end of a field of study. It happens in sports. There is the promise that the right kind of workouts, technique, dedication, and teamwork will produce success, maybe even a championship. It happens in business. There is the enticement that the right kind of work will result in wages, benefits, bonuses, or even promotion. It is used in parenting and even in ministry. Recently, our children's pastor told me that he had used control of the remote for the big screen in children's church as a reward for good attention!

I even read once that it worked (sort of) for a man who wanted to be an Alaskan frontiersman. He was from Oklahoma. He said, "How do I do it? How do I become an Alaskan frontiersman?"

He was told that there were two ways. They said, "We want you to go skin a bear and kiss an Eskimo woman fresh on the lips!"

He said, "I can do it!" He ran out and about a day and a half later he came back. They were shocked! One of his arms was mangled and hanging by his side. He was limping. His eyes were crossed. His hair was down in his face and he said, "*Now where was that Eskimo woman you wanted me to skin!*"

This seems to be the scenario on the day that Peter heard the benefit plan. He believed that the disciples had made great sacrifices and taken great risks and now he wants to know what the reward is.

"Then Peter said in reply, 'See, we have left everything and followed you. What then will we have?'" (Matt. 19:27 ESV).

When Peter asked this question, Jesus told him about a *benefit plan* for those who follow Him. But before understanding this question, we need to understand *the background* of the question that it provided by four previous questions.

The first question comes from a rich young ruler. He wants to know what he can *do* to have eternal life.

I realize that some might read Jesus's response and suggest that Jesus is giving him a "to do" list implying that one can somehow earn eternal life. Clearly, when one examines the life, ministry, and teaching of Jesus, it is clear that He did not believe that you could do any deed that would allow you to earn eternal life. This truth is probably best summarized here:

> Jesus said to him, "I am the way, and the truth, and the life. No one comes to the Father except through me. (John 14:6 ESV)
>
> Jesus does not teach that salvation is ever achieved by divesting oneself of all possessions, even for charitable purposes. However, this youthful inquirer had one concern that was far greater than his desire to have life eternal. His possessions occupied the position of primary devotion in his life. Until he could persuade himself to be willing to seek God regardless of the cost (cf., 6:33), he could never discover eternal life. Therefore, Jesus suggested the selling of his possessions.[47]

Peter was a part of this encounter, and clearly he did not come out of it believing that anyone could do anything to earn eternal life. Here is how he said it as an older man: "Knowing that you were ransomed from the futile ways inherited from your forefathers, not with perishable things such as silver or gold, but with the precious blood of Christ, like that of a lamb without blemish or spot" (1 Pet. 1:18–19 ESV).

The witness of the rest of the New Testament doesn't communicate that anyone can do anything to earn eternal life. For instance, "Now we know that whatever the law says it speaks to those who are under the law, so that every mouth may be stopped, and the whole world may be held accountable to God" (Rom. 3:19–20 ESV).

For by works of the law no human being will be justified in his sight, since through the law comes knowledge of sin.

"For by grace you have been saved through faith. And this is not your own doing; it is the gift of God, not a result of works, so that no one may boast" (Eph. 2:8–9 ESV).

So what is Jesus doing here? He is trying to help this man acknowledge his sin (1 John 1:9) and identify what he truly loves.

"He said to him, 'Which ones?' And Jesus said, 'You shall not murder, You shall not commit adultery, You shall not steal, You shall not bear false witness'" (Matt. 19:18 ESV).

Jesus gives him the moral commands regarding loving your neighbor as yourself. He seems undaunted in his self-righteousness. I wonder if Jesus stops with *bearing false witness* because the man is about to go right ahead and bear false witness! I certainly don't believe him!

"The young man said to him, 'All these I have kept. What do I still lack?'" (Matt. 19:20 ESV).

Now Jesus moves toward what he really loves—his riches. He doesn't do this because there is something inherently wrong with riches. Many of those who have followed the Lord have been wealthy (e.g., Abraham, Lot, David, Solomon, Barnabas, etc.). It is a problem if the wealth has you!

"Jesus said to him, 'If you would be perfect, go, sell what you possess and give to the poor, and you will have treasure in heaven; and come, follow me'" (Matt. 19:21 ESV).

Unfortunately, this man's wealth had him. Wealth can sometimes be the real source of our affections and can hinder our ability to see our need for Jesus. "The young man falls before the commandment 'Thou shalt not covet.' All that the law succeeds in doing is revealing man's sin. His wealth was his security and his god."[48]

The scene is tragic. He went away with his riches and without eternal life and in great sadness. A variety of words are used in the gospels to describe his response. Mark uses the word *stugnazo*, "which appears only two times in the N.T." (Mark 10:22, Matt. 16:3). The literal meaning of the verb is 'be shocked, appalled' or 'be or become gloomy, dark.' The man's dismay and perplexity were evident in his countenance."[49] Luke uses the word *perilupos*, which means "overwhelmingly sad." Matthew uses the word *lupeo*, which means to "be sad."

These three New Testament texts seem to urge us to consider the place of money in our lives and what we really treasure:

> As for the rich in this present age, charge them not to be haughty, nor to set their hopes on the uncertainty of riches, but on God, who richly provides us with everything to enjoy. (1 Tim. 6:17 ESV)

> But those who desire to be rich fall into temptation, into a snare, into many senseless and harmful desires that plunge people into ruin and destruction.
>
> For the love of money is a root of all kinds of evils. It is through this craving that some have wandered away from the faith and pierced themselves with many pangs. (1 Tim. 6:9–10 ESV)

> For where your treasure is, there your heart will be also. (Matt. 6:21 ESV)

As the young man goes away in great sadness, Jesus turns to a truth that He is trying to drive into the lives and perspective of His disciples. That truth is in regard to how difficult it is for the person whose heart is set on riches to enter the kingdom of heaven. Initially, Jesus calls it *hard.* He will later call it *impossible.*

The word for *hard* (*duskolos*) is only used here and in the parallel synoptic accounts (Mark 10:23, Luke 18:24) in all the New Testament.

Jesus then uses hyperbole or exaggeration to make His point. Salvation by human effort is as impossible as a camel going through the eye of a needle. A number of very inventive attempts have been made regarding this but it is best, I think, to simply take it at face value and allow it to say salvation for this rich young ruler or anyone else is *impossible* by human effort. Salvation is a miraculous work of God that can only be received as a gift.

Jesus' response about this encounter stunned the disciples. It went against everything they had been taught. The rich were able to give greater amounts in offerings. They were able to afford the finest sacrificial animals. They appeared to have the blessing of God upon them. To learn that wealth could actually be a *barrier* to God's kingdom was a completely different mindset for them to embrace.

Apparently, Peter did some quick evaluation work regarding what this man had been unwilling to give up versus the disciples giving up everything. And he wants to know what *the benefit plan* is for those who follow Jesus.

For some, this question is almost offensive. They are champions of Ephesians 2:8–9: "For by grace you have been saved through faith. And this is not your own doing; it is the gift of God, not a result of works, so that no one may boast."

But these same folks sometimes seem to be reluctant to champion Ephesians 2:10 as well.

"For we are his workmanship, created in Christ Jesus for good works, which God prepared beforehand, that we should walk in them" (Eph. 2:10 ESV).

We certainly cannot be saved by good works but we *are* saved unto good works. And the investment now of our time, treasure, and talents builds treasure in heaven. In fact, the New Testament makes it clear that our Lord pays careful attention to what is done for Him.

> For God is not unjust so as to overlook your work and the love that you have shown for his name in serving the saints, as you still do. (Heb. 6:10 ESV)

> For a man cannot profit God…but though we are unprofitable to him, our serving him is not unprofitable to us.[50]

> What we need is a big picture of a great God who is utterly committed to joyfully demonstrating His greatness in doing us good.[51]

It is interesting how often during His earthly ministry Jesus talked about reward. Maybe that is the background regarding his question, but clearly, he expected something for those who follow Jesus—*"what will there be for us?"*

I love Jesus' response. The answer is *yes*! There are three wonderful benefits that Jesus shares with Peter. The first is that those who follow Him will also *reign with Him!*

"Jesus said to them, 'Truly, I say to you, in the new world, when the Son of Man will sit on his glorious throne, you who have followed me will also sit on twelve thrones, judging the twelve tribes of Israel'" (Matt. 19:28 ESV).

Of course, this promise is particularly a *benefit* to the twelve. But a similar promise is made to all those who follow the Lord.

"Even when we were dead in our trespasses, made us alive together with Christ—by grace you have been saved—and raised us up with him and seated us with him in the heavenly places in Christ Jesus" (Eph. 2:5–6 ESV).

The second *benefit* that Jesus shared was *rewards*.

"And everyone who has left houses or brothers or sisters or father or mother or children or lands, for my name's sake, will receive a hundredfold and will inherit eternal life" (Matt. 19:29 ESV).

Oh my, what a promise of *reward*! Jesus promises a hundred times as much as what has been given up to follow Him! Years ago, I heard Dr. Bruce Wilkinson say that this represented a 10,000 percent return! Wow!

This language of *reward* occurs often in the balance of the New Testament. Two of my favorite passages are in the book of Hebrews and the book of Revelation.

> And without faith it is impossible to please him, for whoever would draw near to God must believe that he exists and that he rewards those who seek him. (Heb. 11:6 ESV)

> "Behold, I am coming soon! My reward is with me, and I will give to everyone according to what he has done. I am the Alpha and the Omega, the First and the Last, the Beginning and the End." (Rev. 22:12–13 NIV)

I have served for almost three decades in a church that is a short distance from Tinker Air Force Base. Our church has always had a number of government employees, both private sector and military. I still remember the first time one of those employees told me about his benefit plan. At his time of retirement, he would receive somewhere around 80 percent of the three highest earning years of his career for *the rest of his life*! For a pastor who is the son of a construction worker, neither of which had any kind of benefit plan, it blew my mind. I remember thinking, wow—what a benefit plan!

But even that great plan doesn't even come close to what Jesus promises is in store for those who follow Him! Whatever you must give up or have given up to follow Jesus is worth it. He has created you to do good works for His glory. He has an assignment for you. He is paying attention.

I love the way the apostle Paul saw this for his own life.

"But my life is worth nothing to me unless I use it for finishing the work assigned me by the Lord Jesus—the work of telling others the Good News about the wonderful grace of God" (Acts 20:24 NLT).

I also love how he encouraged us to give our best to the work assigned to us.

"Whatever you do, work at it with all your heart, as working for the Lord, not for men" (Col. 3:23 NIV).

Go for it!

9

The Day I Learned the Fig Tree Lesson

Mark 11:20–25
(See also Matt. 21:18–22, Luke 19:45–46)

> As they passed by in the morning, they saw the fig tree withered away to its roots.
>
> And Peter remembered and said to him, "Rabbi, look! The fig tree that you cursed has withered." (Mark 11:20–21 ESV)

This passage reminds me of a TV show that opens with some dramatic scene and then takes us back in time for the context of what is occurring. In this case, we are alerted to it by the words *and Peter remembered* and have to go back to 11:12–14, which is *twenty-four hours earlier.*

The day before, the same fig tree was encountered by a hungry Jesus. Although it was not the season for figs, the tree was in leaf, so fruit was to be expected. Instead, there was none! Jesus cursed the tree because of its fruitlessness.

But for the tree to wither in a twenty-four-hour period was surprising. Typically, a tree would take weeks or months to die, even if it had been salted for the purpose of killing it. This is a supernatural event! In fact, did you know that there are only two occasions in the

Scripture where Jesus uses His miraculous power to do any damage to nature? I'm not even sure that one qualifies—it is where Jesus casts demons into pigs and those pigs run down the slope into the sea and kill themselves. This is the second.

Although this is a literal tree, many believe that it represents Israel, which had an appearance of religion but lacked fruit. Israel is often identified with the fig tree in the Old Testament (see Jer. 8:13, Joel 1:6–7, Hosea 2:12). And Israel, like the fig tree, was barren when Jesus came to it.

Many believe that this is a vivid picture of God's impending judgment on Israel. In this chapter, Jesus rejects Israel's worship by cleansing the temple and then He rejects Israel as a nation by cursing the fig tree. The people apparently get the meaning because they make an amazing turn from the Triumphant Entry to demanding the execution of Jesus!

We must remember that, in the Scripture, *fruit is an indication of life*. Fruit (or lack of it) evidences the root.

> You will recognize them by their fruits. Are grapes gathered from thornbushes, or figs from thistles? (Matt. 7:16 ESV)

> Thus you will recognize them by their fruits. (Matt. 7:20 ESV)

So fruitlessness is very disappointing to Jesus, so much so that He curses the fig tree, and it dies! Jesus then uses hyperbole, an exaggeration for the point of emphasis, to take this fig tree and teach a powerful truth. Clearly, this truth is about believing prayer.

> Therefore I tell you, whatever you ask in prayer. (Mark 11:24a ESV)

> And whenever you stand praying. (Mark 11:25a ESV)

The fig tree lesson is that there is power through believing prayer. "Believing prayer taps God's power to accomplish the humanly impossible."[52]

The point of the hyperbole is not that we are supposed to tell mountains to move, but just as this seems impossible, so our God can accomplish the impossible in response to prayer! But there are two prerequisites (built around three imperatives in the passage) for this kind of *power through prayer*.

The first indispensable element for this kind of power through prayer is *faith* (see also Matthew 17:20).

> And Jesus answered them, "Have faith in God.
>
> Truly, I say to you, whoever says to this mountain, 'Be taken up and thrown into the sea,' and does not doubt in his heart, but believes that what he says will come to pass, it will be done for him.
>
> Therefore I tell you, whatever you ask in prayer, believe that you have received it, and it will be yours." (Mark 11:22–24 ESV)

Here are the first two imperatives: *Have faith in* God and believe. This element is stated negatively—*does not doubt*. And it is stated positively—*believes that what he says will come to pass... believe that you received it*. Jesus begins His answer with—*have faith in God*. Jesus was not suggesting that we have faith in faith or faith in ourselves, but that we have faith in the true and living God—an absolute confidence in Him.

Faith is an indispensable element for the kind of power in prayer that accomplishes the impossible. "Faith accepts it as good as done even though the actual answer is still future."[53] An example of this would be Abraham in Genesis 15. God had promised him that He would bless him with a land. He had promised him that He would bless him with a seed that would become a great nation. And He had promised him that He would bless the world through him (see

Genesis 12:1–3). Now, in Genesis 15, Abram begins to question God regarding the seed. He still has no heir. In response, the Lord takes Abram outside and has him look up to the heavens and encourages him to count the stars and says to him, "so shall your offspring be."

The next words are amazing! The text says, "And he believed the Lord, and he counted it to him as righteousness!" It is as if Abram said, "I need to begin to come up with a lot of names because I am going to have a lot of descendants! God said so!" His faith accepted it as good as done even though the actual answer was still future!

The second indispensable element is *forgiveness.*

"And whenever you stand praying, forgive, if you have anything against anyone, so that your Father also who is in heaven may forgive you your trespasses" (Mark 11:25 ESV).

This is the third imperative of the passage (*forgive*). And it might be more surprising. A prerequisite for this kind of power in prayer is forgiveness. God empowers those who forgive. He moves on their behalf.

I just finished reading the story of evangelist Josh McDowell. As the book says, it is "one man's real-life journey from unspeakable memories to unbelievable grace."[54] One element of the book is the story of Josh expressing forgiveness to his father who had been abusive to both he and his mother during years of drunkenness. That forgiveness opened the door for God to do a mighty work in the heart of his dad. It culminated like this:

> "Josh," he said, "if Jesus can do for me what I've seen Him do in your life, then I want to know Him."
>
> Now it was my turn to cry. "You need to ask Him into your life, Dad. You need to open your heart to Him and pray."
>
> "I don't reckon I know how to pray, son."
>
> "Just tell Him what's in your heart."
>
> Dad nodded and said a simple, down-to-earth prayer, a "farmer's prayer," if you will. "God, if You are God, and if Christ is Your Son…and

> if You can forgive me for what I've done to my family…" His voice broke. He composed himself and sighing deeply, prayed the heartrending words, "And if You can do in my life what I've seen You do in my son's life, then please…" Dad struck his chest and cried out, "Please come in!"[55]
>
> McDowell goes on to say, "You know, when a person gives his or her life to Christ, everything changes. When I made that commitment, my attitude and actions began to change over a period of a year and a half. But when my father came to Christ, the transformation was immediate. He changed right in front of me! It was as if someone reached down inside him and turned on a switch that flooded light into a dark room."[56]

Because he had forgiven, he had the privilege of seeing His God do the impossible. God had moved the mountain and completely changed his dad's life and eternity!

I think it is also important to remember that this kind of power in prayer is responding to and trusting in the revealed will of God. I like the way that John MacArthur Jr. says it, "The believer who wants what God wants can ask from God and receive it."[57]

> And this is the confidence that we have toward him, that if we ask anything according to his will he hears us. (John 5:14 ESV)

> Pray then like this: "Our Father in heaven, hallowed be your name.
>
> Your kingdom come, your will be done, on earth as it is in heaven. (Matt. 6:9–10 ESV)

> And he said, "'Abba, Father, all things are possible for you. Remove this cup from me. Yet

> not what I will, but what you will." (Mark 14:36 ESV)

The *fig tree lesson* is that there is power in prayer. It is prayer that is an expression of *faith*, focused on the revealed will of God, from a person who is a forgiven one who *forgives* others. God responds to this kind of prayer in such a way that He accomplishes the impossible!

Of course, this begs the question: how does God reveal His will? I think the three primary answers to that question are: (1) the revelation of His Word, (2) the voice of His Spirit; (3) the counsel of His people. Therefore, to know the revealed will of God that I am to focus on by faith in prayer—I must be in His Word, listening to the voice of His Spirit, and engaged with His people!

That brings me to the words *stand praying*. BAGD says that the word *stand* here can mean "to be in a standing position or to be firmly committed in conviction or belief." In light of the context, I suggest that it is the second meaning here. It is the man or woman who has heard from God and by faith he or she stands firmly committed in belief that God will accomplish what He has revealed in response to his or her prayer!

In the spring of 1984, my wife and I were young twenty-six-year-olds with a one-and-a-half-year-old little boy. I had resigned my ministry position at the church we had been serving and was working for an electrical company at $6 an hour. My wife was a stay-at-home mom. Although we were extremely frugal, we were slowly dying financially.

The church we began to attend hosted evangelist Manley Beasley for a week. We did not miss a service. We were desperate to hear from God. He spent the entire week preaching about *faith*. I later learned that many in Southern Baptist life called him the apostle of faith.

One night, Manley said something I had never heard anyone say, nor have I ever heard it again. He said, "Some of you have a financial need. As an expression of faith, you need to tithe on that need."

In a way that I rarely have, in my forty plus years as a Christ-follower, I sensed the Spirit of God prompting me to respond by faith. I approached my wife about it, and she agreed. We had a $5,000 need. At that time in our lives it might as well have been a $5,000,000 need.

It was one of the scariest moments of my life as we wrote a check that night for $500. It emptied our account. We had nothing but what we believed we had heard from God. If He didn't do the impossible, we were sunk.

In the next two weeks, the Lord caused a series of events to happen and the impossible happened! I will never forget driving down the interstate the day that it all culminated holding a $5,000 check in my hand! It was one of the greatest times of worship in my life as I wept and proclaimed the greatness of my God who had done what seemed impossible on our behalf!

Peter saw it that day when he learned *the fig tree lesson.* I wonder if every time he walked by a fig tree, he thought of it again! He learned that there is power in prayer offered by faith with a forgiving heart.

10

The Day Jesus Washed My Feet

John 13:1–17

I don't know about you, but when I think about beautiful things, feet don't rank very high on my list. Feet are sweaty and can be stinky. Did you know that your feet have roughly 250,000 sweat glands and that they excrete as much as half a pint of moisture each day?![58] No wonder they can be stinky!

I read that Madeline Albrecht really knows about stinky feet. Madeline knew she was destined for greatness when she was hired by the Hill Top Research Laboratories, a testing lab for Dr. Scholl's. Her job was to sniff feet, which she did for fifteen years. During her pungent career, Madeline set the world record for sniffing approximately 5,600 feet.[59] You thought your job stinks!

In 2015, a wonderful movie on the power of prayer was released called *War Room*. I was amused that the writers must not have considered feet very beautiful as well. Throughout the movie, attention is made over and over to the smelliness of the feet of the character played by Priscilla Shirer. Toward the end of the movie her husband washes her feet while *wearing a painter's mask*!

I doubt that her feet could have been anywhere near what a first-century disciple's feet were like. The conditions of the day were difficult and unsanitary. They walked everywhere they went. The roads weren't paved. When I delivered this part of Peter's adventure to the people I pastor, I showed them several pictures of feet that I discovered via Google. One was a picture of a very pretty set of lady's feet in high heels. Another was a set of feet that were so damaged that they were blackened and the nails were deformed. A third picture was of some incredibly hairy feet. The final picture was feet that might have resembled the disciples' feet in the first century—sandalled and muddy.

In this part of his adventure with Jesus, Peter has an encounter that involved his feet. And he learned a lot. So should we.

This part of Peter's adventure happens just before the Passover Feast. It is during the evening meal and is a lavish display of Jesus' love for His disciples.

"Now before the Feast of the Passover, when Jesus knew that his hour had come to depart out of this world to the Father, having loved his own who were in the world, he loved them to the end" (John 13:1 ESV).

Jesus displayed His love by washing their feet. As He came to Peter there is an interchange that has often confused those who read it.

> He came to Simon Peter, who said to him, "Lord, do you wash my feet?"
>
> Jesus answered him, "What I am doing you do not understand now, but afterward you will understand."
>
> Peter said to him, "You shall never wash my feet." Jesus answered him, "If I do not wash you, you have no share with me."
>
> Simon Peter said to him, "Lord, not my feet only but also my hands and my head!"
>
> Jesus said to him, "The one who has bathed does not need to wash, except for his feet, but is completely clean. And you are clean, but not every one of you." (John 13:6–10 ESV)

The confusion goes away though with an understanding of two words used here in the original. The first word is the word *nipto.* It is used in verses 5, 6, 8, 10, 12, and 14. It means "to wash a part of the body."

The second word is the word *louo*. It is only used in verse 10, but its distinction is important in understanding the text. It means "to bathe all over." It is also important to note that it is a perfect passive participle. It is a bathing being done in the past to the recipient with ongoing results. It would be translated *having been bathed all over*. It is intended to point to a bathing that is settled once and for all.

With that background into the text, and sticking with the feet, I believe that when Jesus washed his feet Peter learned that he had to look *beyond* his feet. He had to consider whether or not he had experienced *a washing of regeneration*—a once and for all, settled, *bathing of the life* producing salvation.

"He saved us, not because of works done by us in righteousness, but according to his own mercy, by the washing of regeneration and renewal of the Holy Spirit" (Titus 3:5 ESV).

Jesus said that all of them except Judas had experienced this cleansing. It is *relational* and settled and never has to be repeated.

Peter also learned that he had to look *at* his feet. He learned that even though one has been cleansed in this relational way, his feet can get dirty as he walks through this sin-stained life. That daily dirt (sin) affects our *fellowship* with the Lord and needs to be cleansed (confessed) on a daily basis. This is present tense language in the original. It is describing an ongoing, daily need for confession and forgiveness. It is expressed well in John's first epistle.

"If we confess our sins, he is faithful and just to forgive us our sins and to cleanse us from all unrighteousness" (1 John 1:9 ESV).

The dialogue between Jesus and Peter, beginning in verse 8, is fabulous, as Jesus highlights this need for daily cleansing. Let me give it to you noting the words we have discussed.

> Peter said to him, "You shall never wash (nipto) my feet." Jesus answered him, "If I do not wash (nipto) you, you have no share with me."
>
> Simon Peter said to him, "Lord, not my feet only but also my hands and my head!"
>
> Jesus said to him, "The one who has bathed (louo) does not need to wash (nipto), except for

> his feet, but is completely clean. And you are clean, but not every one of you." (John 13:8–10 ESV)

Finally, Peter learned that he had to *use* his feet because Jesus clearly had a mission for His men.

> When he had washed their feet and put on his outer garments and resumed his place, he said to them, "Do you understand what I have done to you?
>
> You call me Teacher and Lord, and you are right, for so I am.
>
> If I then, your Lord and Teacher, have washed your feet, you also ought to wash one another's feet.
>
> For I have given you an example, that you also should do just as I have done to you.
>
> Truly, truly, I say to you, a servant is not greater than his master, nor is a messenger greater than the one who sent him. (John 13:12–16 ESV)

He had given them an example. And what Jesus had done as an example, He wanted His followers to do for others. And He promised blessings upon those who did so! We are to use our feet to *serve* others. We are *indebted* to do it ("you also ought")!

As I said, He had given them an example. And note the words, "that you also should do just as I have done to you." What had Jesus done here? He had helped his men regarding their need for daily cleansing from sin. I think He is saying that we, too, are to be so engaged in the lives of others that we assist our brothers and sisters in their need for daily cleansing from sin. I believe that these two New Testament passages declare this as well:

> Therefore, confess your sins to one another and pray for one another, that you may be healed.

> The prayer of a righteous person has great power as it is working. (James 5:16 ESV)

> Brothers, if anyone is caught in any transgression, you who are spiritual should restore him in a spirit of gentleness. Keep watch on yourself, lest you too be tempted. (Gal. 6:1 ESV)

There needs to be such a relationship between us, as followers of Christ, that we could feel the freedom and confidence that we could go to each other in honesty regarding sin and anticipate assistance and encouragement toward cleansing of sin. In the church, our groups must be more than study groups (although studying the Word of God is incredibly important). They must be places of community where lives are shared.

Jesus's example also involves *service*. He stooped to serve their need. He came for this very purpose.

"For even the Son of Man came not to be served but to serve, and to give his life as a ransom for many" (Mark 10:45 ESV).

I am embarrassed to say how many times through my years as a Christ-follower that I have *not* followed Jesus's example as I should have. Too often it wasn't about others. Too often I have failed to serve because it was all about me.

One of those times that I deeply regret happened in the very early years of ministry, before Mellanie and I had any children. A young, single woman in our church invited us to her home for lunch, after our morning service. She was not only young and single, she was also bordering on being impoverished. It was an incredible sacrifice for her to have us over and feed us.

Frankly, I wasn't all that excited about the invitation. My Sundays were incredibly busy with ministry responsibility. And back then, I thought I had to watch Sunday afternoon NFL football.

There is no telling what kind of sacrifice it took for that dear lady to host us. But I was not interested in being there long. I was rude. I was ungrateful. I was more interested in my needs than about hers. *How dare I!* The Spirit of God broke my heart over this sometime later. He has also reminded me of it over the years as He attempts to cause growth in my life that would help me serve others more like my Master.

It would be so much better if our view was that we have been so privileged to be loved by a Great Savior, and I want my life, like His, to be used in the service of others.

> Shane Claiborne, who spent a summer in the slums of Calcutta with Mother Teresa, wrote the following about one of his experiences:
>
> 'People often ask me what Mother Teresa was like. Did she glow in the dark or have a halo? She was short, wrinkled, and precious, maybe even a little ornery—like a beautiful, wise old granny.
>
> But there is one thing I will never forget—her feet were deformed. Each morning during Mass, I would stare at those feet. I wondered if Mother Teresa had leprosy. But I wasn't going to ask, of course.
>
> One day a sister asked us, "Have you noticed Mother's feet?" We nodded, curious. She said, "Her feet are deformed because we get just enough donated shoes for everyone, and Mother does not want anyone to get stuck with the worst pair, so she digs through and finds those. Years of wearing bad shoes have deformed her feet."[60]

Her feet were deformed in the service of others! Are you using your feet in the service of others? This is what Jesus desires of those who follow Him.

I would like to offer one last thought about our *feet*—we can have beautiful feet! There are at least two ways to have them. One is through *serving others* as this text has taught us. The second way is by *engaging others with the good news!*

> How beautiful upon the mountains are the feet of him who brings good news, who publishes

peace, who brings good news of happiness, who publishes salvation, who says to Zion, "Your God reigns." (Isa. 52:7 ESV)

And how are they to preach unless they are sent? As it is written, "How beautiful are the feet of those who preach the good news!" (Rom. 10:15 ESV)

11

The Day I Made a Promise (I Could Not Keep)

Selected Passages

I am a huge *Andy Griffith Show* fan. In an episode called "The Pagent," the character Barney Fife shows off his dexterity of tongue by rattling off several tongue twisters for Andy's son Opie. But when he is challenged by Andy with a new one, he opens his mouth and fails miserably. It is a humorous reminder that our mouths can really go awry.

In this famous episode of Peter's adventure with Jesus, he opens his mouth with great bravado and makes a *promise he could not keep*. Let's look first at his *declaration*.

> And Jesus said to them, "You will all fall away, for it is written, 'I will strike the shepherd, and the sheep will be scattered.'
>
> But after I am raised up, I will go before you to Galilee."
>
> Peter said to him, "Even though they all fall away, I will not."

> And Jesus said to him, "Truly, I tell you, this very night, before the rooster crows twice, you will deny me three times."
>
> But he said emphatically, "If I must die with you, I will not deny you." And they all said the same. (Mark 14:27–31 ESV; see also Matthew 26:31–35, Luke 22:24–34, John 13:36–38)

Peter's *declaration* is, "Even though they all fall away, I will not." It is incredible boasting on Peter's part. It must have been greatly offensive to the other disciples. It is easy to see the flesh here as Peter says, "Even though *they all* fall away, *I will not*" (v. 29).

Matthew's account reads much like the Mark account: "If I must die with you, I will not deny you."

John's account says, "I will lay down my life for you."

In Luke's account, we are given the amazing context of this *declaration*. Jesus had been talking to His men about His death, and they are in the midst of a dispute about which of them was the greatest!

Jesus not only makes it clear that Peter will not be able to fulfill his promise, he also gives a very specific time frame that his denial will occur by referencing the rooster crowing twice. Remember that the night was divided up into four watches with a trumpet blast signaling both the beginning and the ending of each watch. This is made clear for us both historically and in Mark's gospel.

"Therefore stay awake—for you do not know when the master of the house will come, in the evening, or at midnight, or when the rooster crows, or in the morning" (Mark 13:35 ESV).

The second scene of the promise that Peter could not keep is a scene of *danger* (see Matthew 26:47–56, Mark 14:43–50, Luke 22:47–53, John 18:1–11).

"Then Simon Peter, having a sword, drew it and struck the high priest's servant and cut off his right ear" (John 18:10–11 ESV). (The servant's name was Malchus.)

So Jesus said to Peter, "Put your sword into its sheath; shall I not drink the cup that the Father has given me?"

To his credit, Peter attempts to act upon his declaration by pulling a sword against a detachment of soldiers and officials of the chief priests and Pharisees who were carrying weapons (John 18:3). Matthew and Mark tell us that he cut off the ear of the assaulted man. Luke tells us it was the right ear. John tells us that his name was Malchus.

It is fascinating that, according to John, this whole thing occurred in the context of Jesus declaring Himself as the I AM (literal Greek translation) and attempting to guard the safety of His men. Peter put everyone in *danger* by his act! Jesus quickly ends the *danger* by having Peter put away the sword and demanding "no more of this" (Luke 22:51). And then He healed Malchus's ear (Luke 22:51)! Isn't it amazing that at the conclusion of a miracle that we read, "then seizing him, they led him away" (Luke 22:54)? Such is the depravity and darkness of mankind that it responds to miraculous goodness with evil and hatred!

It is in the moments that follow that we observe Peter's *denial.* Before going too far, it seems prudent to remind ourselves that Peter was not the only one who denied the Lord.

"'But all this has taken place that the Scriptures of the prophets might be fulfilled.' Then all the disciples left him and fled" (Matt. 26:56 ESV).

And to his credit, he and John are the only two who returned to see what would happen to Jesus.

"Simon Peter followed Jesus and so did another disciple. Since that disciple was known to the high priest, he entered with Jesus into the courtyard of the high priest" (John 18:15 ESV).

Actually, it is interesting to me to note how each of the Gospels details these three *episodes of denials* (see Matthew 26:69–75, Mark 14:66–72, Luke 22:54–62, John 18:15–27).

John: First, the girl at the door.

Second, presumably the servants and officials around a fire—"they."

Third...one (singular) of the high priest's servants, a relative of Malchus.

Luke: First, a servant girl seated in the firelight.
Second, someone else (a man).
Third, another (singular).
Mark: First, a servant girl.
Second, the *same* servant girl.
Third, those (plural) standing near.
Matthew: First, a servant girl.
Second, *another* girl.
Third, those (plural) standing there.

Each Gospel writer details three *denials*, but there are clearly differences. Peter certainly denied the Lord at least three times and putting all these accounts together may suggest that there were three *episodes* of denials that involved a variety of people. It appears that Peter was denying the Lord *all over the place*!

Peter had made a great promise, but sadly, he couldn't keep it. I see this episode in his adventure with Jesus as a great admonishment about our moments of bravado. I believe there are great lessons to learn. For instance, it is a great reminder that *acts in the flesh can cause unwise proclamations*. Peter was full of himself and confident in his own abilities. That is a dangerous place for any of us. I cannot think of one occasion where I have spoken in the flesh that I am not ashamed of—not one! How about you? When the flesh reigns, it is just not pretty!

It is also a warning that *acts in the flesh can get you and others hurt*. Peter put everyone at risk. Had the Savior not stepped in, who knows what would have happened. He put everyone in danger and so can we when we act in the flesh. I was telling a friend lately about getting "flipped off" repeatedly because I had the audacity to drive the speed limit, and I got in their way. My friend said that he tells his grandchildren, in light of the day in which we live, that if someone did something similar to them, they were to keep their hands on their steering wheel, keep their hands off the horn, and to keep their mouth shut! He is trying to help them not respond in the flesh and potentially get hurt! It is good advice!

And there is a grave warning here that *acts in the flesh can take you to places you would have never imagined.* Peter never thought he would be denying that he even knew Jesus. He never thought he would be making that denial by cursing, unacceptable language. He never thought he would find himself hearing a signal for the changing of the guard and looking straight into the eyes of a disappointed Savior and be broken by his betrayal!

> But Peter said, "Man, I do not know what you are talking about." And immediately, while he was still speaking, the rooster crowed.
>
> And the Lord turned and looked at Peter. And Peter remembered the saying of the Lord, how he had said to him, "Before the rooster crows today, you will deny me three times."
>
> And he went out and wept bitterly. (Luke 22:60–62 ESV)

So in our own adventure with Jesus we must *beware* of the pride that often accompanies being in the flesh. We must beware ever putting confidence in the flesh. These passages affirm this caution:

> Pride goes before destruction, and a haughty spirit before a fall. (Prov. 16:18 ESV)

> When pride comes, then comes disgrace, but with the humble is wisdom. (Prov. 11:2 ESV)

> For we are the circumcision, who worship by the Spirit of God and glory in Christ Jesus and put no confidence in the flesh. (Phil. 3:3 ESV)

We must not only make sure in our adventure with Jesus we beware of pride, we must also live our adventure in *belief.* Our adventure needs to be characterized by living a life of faith.

"I have been crucified with Christ. It is no longer I who live, but Christ who lives in me. And the life I now live in the flesh *I live by faith* in the Son of God, who loved me and gave himself for me" (Gal. 2:20 ESV).

Finally, I think that this episode in the life of Peter urges us to *be balanced.* I believe that these two passages of Scripture present the kind of balance you and I should aim at.

> I am the vine; you are the branches. Whoever abides in me and I in him, he it is that bears much fruit, for apart from me you can do nothing. (John 15:5 ESV)

> I can do all things through him who strengthens me. (Phil. 4:13 ESV)

It is my hope for my life, as well as yours, that this kind of balance produces a genuine humility and dependence in our lives, coupled with a quiet confidence in the Christ who has invaded our lives in the person of the Holy Spirit.

In the eighteenth century, that balance was put on display by George Whitfield. As you may remember, Whitfield was a Calvinist and John Wesley was an Arminian. Their theological views were therefore in conflict and sometimes hotly debated by them or those who adhered to their positions.

On one occasion, one of Whitfield's followers is reported to have said to Whitfield, "We won't see Wesley in heaven, will we?" To which Whitfield is said to have replied, "You're right, we won't see him in heaven. He'll be so close to the throne of God, that we won't be able to see him!"

What humility and absence of the pride of the flesh! May that be you and I throughout our adventure with Jesus instead of making a bunch of the promises in the flesh, full of ourselves, that we won't be able to keep!

The day I made a promise (I could not keep)

12

The Lesser Light

John 1:35–42

Let's pause for a moment regarding these *days* in Peter's adventure with Jesus and look back at where the adventure began and the life that, I'm convinced, Peter would never forget!

"One of the two who heard John speak and followed Jesus was Andrew, Simon Peter's brother" (John 1:40 ESV).

That life was Peter's brother, Andrew. He was apparently one of the first two disciples of Jesus. Some have said that this was recognized by the early church, who gave him the title *protokletos*, which means "first-called."

But he never rose to prominence like Peter. If Peter was a great light for Christianity, Andrew was a *lesser light*.

In describing his brother, I believe that Peter would say that Andrew was *an average man*. I love the way R. Kent Hughes puts it:

> It is highly significant that Andrew, one of the names most associated with witness in the Bible, was an average man who shared Christ in patently ordinary ways. In fact, there appears to be some intentional divine poetry in his name, for "Andrew" comes from the Greek root *andros*, which means, "man." Thus, he is an example

> for everyone who would follow Christ. Andrew is what every man ought to be in witnessing for Christ. Thus, a glance at his life will properly challenge and motivate us all.[61]

I believe that Peter would also say that his brother was *a spiritually sensitive man.* I think this because of how we encounter him in this passage. When he first met Jesus, he had already been engaged in the ministry of John the Baptist.

> The next day again John was standing with two of his disciples,
>
> and he looked at Jesus as he walked by and said, "Behold, the Lamb of God!"
>
> The two disciples heard him say this, and they followed Jesus.
>
> Jesus turned and saw them following and said to them, "What are you seeking?" And they said to him, "Rabbi" (which means Teacher), "where are you staying?"
>
> He said to them, "Come and you will see." So they came and saw where he was staying, and they stayed with him that day, for it was about the tenth hour. (John 1:35–39 ESV)

This means that he recognized that he lived in evil days. It meant he had been baptized in repentance of sin. And clearly, he was looking for the coming Messiah, so it was easy for John to point him to the Lamb of God. This all implies that he was spiritually sensitive and responsive, quick to pursue the things of God.

Finally, I think that Peter would say that his brother Andrew was *an intentionally engaging man.*

"He first found his own brother Simon and said to him, 'We have found the Messiah' (which means Christ)" (John 1:41 ESV).

He never reached a prominent position among the followers of Jesus. He was never in the inner circle like Peter, James, and John.

He, therefore, missed many of the experiences of Peter discussed in this book. He never preached a sermon that God saw fit to record. He wrote no New Testament letters. It is never recorded that God used him like his brother in the performance of a miracle.

As near as we can tell, he did one thing well—he intentionally engaged others for the purpose of bringing them to Christ! I had a teacher years ago who described Andrew like the "pilot light" on a stove. Peter was the great bright fire for Christ. Andrew was simply the "pilot light" that the Lord used to ignite the great flame!

It reminds me of Anne Sullivan's impact on Helen Keller and her subsequent impact on the world. And it reminds me of Edward Kimball, the almost unknown Sunday School teacher, who presented Christ to the young shoe salesman, D. L. Moody, and was used of God to ignite a flaming evangelist that would have incredible impact for the kingdom of God.

What an impact Andrew had because a priority of his life was to engage in spiritual conversations with those around him. He intentionally engaged others for the cause of Christ. He was used of God to shake the world as a result!

I love the way this impact is described by R. Kent Hughes who says that the grand distinction is that he excelled in bringing others to Christ:

> Has endeared him to whole cultures so that today he is the patron saint of three diverse nations. Eusebius in his *Ecclesiastical History* alleges that Andrew later went to Scythia, the country north of the Black Sea between the Danube and Tanais Rivers, which today is part of modern Russia. Another tradition makes him the patron saint of Greece, for it says that he was martyred there on an X-shaped cross, where he hung for three days praising God and praying for his enemies. The third country which claims Andrew is Scotland, on the fanciful supposition that after the eight-century monk Regulus

> brought Andrew's relics (three fingers from his right hand, an arm bone, one tooth, and a kneecap) to what is today St. Andrew's, Scotland, the Scots were led into battle by a white X-shaped cross levitating above them in the blue sky. Since then, the white St. Andrew's cross on a sky-blue background has been the standard of Scotland.
>
> Did Andrew actually go to Greece or Russia or Scotland? No one knows. Why do three countries, therefore, claim him? The answer rests in Andrew's winsome character as it is recorded in Scripture. He was a great-hearted man of average abilities who loved to introduce others to Christ. Average Andrew's extraordinary evangelistic heart has made his name one of such fadeless beauty that whole nations want to claim him.[62]

He was, early on, exactly what Jesus would want His men to be—a witness. And Peter was forever impacted by a brother who would simply engage him with the Messiah he had found!

"But you will receive power when the Holy Spirit has come upon you, and you will be my witnesses" (Acts 1:8 ESV).

May the life and legacy of Andrew encourage you and me to look for opportunities to engage in spiritual conversations where we might tell our story of the Messiah we have found. May we do so at every opportunity because it is a priority of our life.

"The fruit of the righteous is a tree of life, And he who wins souls is wise" (Prov. 11:30 NKJV).

The lesser light.

13

The Day at the Tomb

John 20:1–9

We get some background to this episode of Peter's adventure from Mark 16:9 concerning what the disciples are feeling and their emotional state. Mark says that the disciples are "mourning and weeping." They are devastated. Their idea of the Messiah has perished with Jesus at the cross. They are still clueless in regard to the resurrection (John 20:9), although, by my count, Jesus had told them five times that He would rise from the dead! They are devastated, disillusioned, and disappointed as we encounter this scene.

This part of Peter's adventure comprises some of the most poignant evidence that a supernatural resurrection had occurred. When Peter and John looked into the tomb, which they found vacant, their attention was held by the empty mummy wrap and the head piece set off by itself.

Their journey to the tomb had been prompted by Mary Magdalene, who had gone to the tomb early that morning and discovered that the stone had been removed from the entrance. She had run to Peter and John and told them what she saw with the added statement assuming that the body had been taken. It is interesting that although Jesus had predicted His resurrection many times, it was beyond comprehension to His followers. For most of them it would take "many convincing proofs" (Acts 1:3) for them to grasp that He was alive.

As we observe the two disciples running to the tomb, there are some important words that we will encounter. They are words that have to do with looking at something or seeing. They are key to understanding the text.

"Now on the first day of the week Mary Magdalene came to the tomb early, while it was still dark, and *saw* that the stone had been taken away from the tomb" (John 20:1–5 ESV).

So she ran and went to Simon Peter and the other disciple, the one whom Jesus loved, and said to them, "They have taken the Lord out of the tomb, and we do not know where they have laid him."

So Peter went out with the other disciple, and they were going toward the tomb.

Both of them were running together, but the other disciple outran Peter and reached the tomb first.

And stooping to look in, he *saw* the linen cloths lying there, but he did not go in.

The first of these words that we encounter is the word *blepo*. It occurs in both verse 1 and verse 5. It is a general word for "see." This is a *casual glance*. Mary observed the moved stone early that morning and ran to the disciples. John had stooped to look in and his casual glance had observed something more, the linen cloths lying there. He probably thought that Mary had made a mistake as he observed the graveclothes lying on the stone shelf without any appearance of anyone doing anything to them.

The next mention of sight involves a more *careful attention* as Peter went into the tomb.

"Then Simon Peter came, following him, and went into the tomb. He *saw* the linen cloths lying there, and the face cloth, which had been on Jesus's head, not lying with the linen cloths but folded up in a place by itself" (John 20:6–7 ESV).

This is the word *theoreo* and means "to observe something with sustained attention, be a spectator, look at, or observe." The word means that Peter theorized regarding or paid careful attention for the purpose of comprehending the significance of what he was observing. And apparently, what he was observing was the still intact graveclothes without a body inside!

John MacArthur puts it this way,

> A contrast existed between the resurrection of Lazarus (11:44) and that of Jesus. While Lazarus came forth from the grave wearing his graveclothes, Jesus' body, though physical and material, was glorified and was now able to pass through the graveclothes much in the same way that He later appeared in the locked room (see vv. 19, 20)...the state of the items indicates no struggle, no hurried unwrapping of the body by grave robbers, who wouldn't unwrap the body anyway, since transporting it elsewhere would be easier and more pleasant if it was left in its unwrapped and spiced condition. All appearances indicated that no one had taken the body, but that it had moved through the cloth and left it behind in the tomb.[63]

I realize that you might say at this point, "Pastor, do you really believe something like that?" My answer is, "yes, I do." The resurrection body of Jesus was very different than ours. In fact, notice these words just a few verses later in John 20: "On the evening of that day, the first day of the week, the doors being locked where the disciples were for fear of the Jews, Jesus came and stood among them and said to them, 'Peace be with you'" (John 20:19 ESV).

Jesus appears to His men by going *right through* locked doors in His resurrected body! It is a feature of the resurrected body. Passing through these linen cloths would be no challenge at all!

The third Greek word for seeing in this passage occurs in verse 8. This results in *committed belief*.

"Then the other disciple, who had reached the tomb first, also went in, and he *saw* and believed; for as yet they did not understand the Scripture, that he must rise from the dead" (John 20:8–9 ESV).

This is the word *eidon* and comes from *horao*. It means "to see with perception." Or, as Warren Wiersbe puts it, "to perceive with intelligent comprehension."[64] It results in John believing. I appreciate G. L. Borchert's observation regarding John's belief. "It is particularly noteworthy that the beloved disciple is the only person in the Gospels who is recognized as having reached a point of believing as the result of seeing the empty tomb."[65] John went in and saw the same thing Peter did, but the light came on for John and he believed!

The passage ends this way, "then the disciples went back to their homes." John went home believing. How did Peter go home? Luke tells us.

"But Peter rose and ran to the tomb; stooping and looking in, he saw the linen cloths by themselves; and he went home *marveling* at what had happened" (Luke 24:12 ESV).

The word *marveling* is the word *thaumadzo* and means "to be extraordinarily impressed or disturbed by something, to wonder, marvel, or be astonished." Luke used it a number of times in his gospel:

- Verse 1:63, the naming of John.
- Verse 2:18, the response to the proclamation of the shepherds.
- Verse 2:33, the marveling of Joseph and Mary at what is being said about Jesus.
- Verse 4:22, marveling at Jesus' gracious words.
- Verse 8:25, the disciples' response to the winds and waves obeying Jesus.
- Verse 11:14, response to the speech of the man who had previously been demonically mute.
- Verse 24:41, the response of the disciples to the appearance of the resurrected Christ.

Peter left the tomb that day astonished and marveling at what he saw. I believe that there are at least three words of application for us today that Peter might say as he asks us to *look into that tomb and marvel*:

1. I believe that he would ask us to *embrace the reality of the human condition*. We are indeed *all* sinners, separated from a holy God. There has been an awful price paid that there might be forgiveness for our rebellion against a holy God! We should be ever moved by the cost!
2. I believe that he would ask us to *embrace the reality of the payment*. The resurrection screams that the payment for our sin was accepted! We can be accepted and forgiven in Christ! To live without faith in the resurrection is to deny biblical evidence. To die without hope of the resurrection is to face a barren eternity.
3. Finally, I believe that Peter would ask us to *embrace the reality of the living Savior*. I think he would urge us to not be "slow of heart" to believe (Luke 24:25), but to be like John, who, in comparison to the other disciples was quick to believe even though he had stood at the cross (John 19:26) and personally observed the death of Jesus.

I like the way that Alfred Ackley said it in 1933: [66]

> I serve a risen Savior, he's in the world today;
> I know that he is living, whatever men may say;
> I see his hand of mercy, I hear his voice of cheer, and just the time I need him he's always near.
> He lives, he lives, Christ Jesus lives today! He walks with me and talks with me along life's narrow way.
> He lives, he lives, salvation to impart! You ask me how I know he lives: he lives within my heart.

I also like the way singer/songwriter Luke Garrett put it in one line of a song he recorded about twenty years ago: "He's not sealed up in a tomb, He's alive and in this room!"

The day at the tomb.

14

The Day I Had Breakfast with Jesus

John 21

I love John 21. One of the reasons is that when I was about twenty-two years of age, I took a group of students on a five-state choir tour. It was at my first church. We went in an old broken-down bus. In fact, it broke down on us on our way home. I had to hitch hike into the nearest town to get help fixing it. You can imagine my surprise when I arrived back at the bus to find two of our male students on top of the bus sun tanning! The musical that we did on that tour was called *Breakfast in Galilee.* It was built around John 21.

This next encounter with Peter is after the tomb experience as Jesus is revealing Himself to His disciples for the third time (21:14, the reference to the "third time" refers only to the appearances reported in John's gospel, i.e., the first being in 20:19–23, and the second in 20:26–29).

Jesus is soon to ascend. He is preparing to release His men to their mission of making disciples. This is a critical meeting and Mark tells us that He has specifically mentioned Peter (remember, Peter would have the keys, Matthew 16:18).

"But go, tell his disciples *and Peter* that he is going before you to Galilee. There you will see him, just as he told you" (Mark 16:7 ESV).

The events of the meeting were impacting. John records vivid details, such as how far they were from land (two hundred cubits, verse 8); the fish and bread on the fire of coals (verse 9); and the number of large fish caught (153, verse 11).

These vivid memories are the second reason that I love John 21. Remember, it happened just as day was breaking (21:4) and it happened at the Sea of Galilee (which is really a lake). As a child my dad worked lots of hours to try to provide for us. Sometimes he would work twelve hour shifts for all seven days of the week, which meant that I rarely saw him. On the rare occasions that he would get a weekend off, we would sometimes go to a lake. As daylight would arrive, I would be up, and my dad was kind enough to get up with me and would begin to pull me as I skied behind our boat.

My mom would begin to prepare an amazing breakfast over open fire or a Coleman stove that would be waiting for us when we returned!

My dad was kind enough to pull me until I was tired, or we were about out of gas. The memories are so vivid. The water was usually like glass that time of morning, and as I crossed wakes my skies would make this distinct sound that I still hear. And I can almost still smell the incredible aroma of that breakfast, as we made our way back to the camp! What great memories!

It seems significant that Jesus wanted to share this meal with them. Then, as now, sharing a meal was meaningful. It involved community and shared life. Remember that being with Him was central to Jesus's method of producing disciples.

"And he appointed twelve (whom he also named apostles) so *that they might be with him* and he might send them out to preach" (Mark 3:14 ESV).

It was such a marvelous invitation as Jesus will ultimately invite them to "come and dine" (21:12, Luke 5:1–11). Surely, this event would have flooded them with memories. It would have been a *de ja vu* moment. Have you ever had one of those? I have had several in my life. One of those occurred in my twenties.

As a child my family traveled all over Oklahoma because my dad worked for a road construction company. One of the towns we lived in was Valliant. I think I was in the third grade during the three months or so we lived there.

In my twenties, I was an assistant football coach and our team traveled to Valliant, Oklahoma, to play them. I really hadn't thought much (if at all) about going back to a place I had lived as a child.

Before the game, we were to dress out in an older gym and my responsibility included taping our players ankles. I was busy doing that in that old gym when I looked up and suddenly realized that it was the very gym I had played in as a child! It was an interesting moment!

I think that Peter and the others would have been reminded of their initial calling.

> Passing alongside the Sea of Galilee, he saw Simon and Andrew the brother of Simon casting a net into the sea, for they were fishermen.
>
> And Jesus said to them, "Follow me, and I will make you become fishers of men."
>
> And immediately they left their nets and followed him.
>
> And going on a little farther, he saw James the son of Zebedee and John his brother, who were in their boat mending the nets.
>
> And immediately he called them, and they left their father Zebedee in the boat with the hired servants and followed him. (Mark 1:16–20 ESV; see also Luke 5:1–11)

It seems to me that it would have been impossible to miss the location, the fishing, that they had caught nothing, and the large catch after obeying Jesus! I also don't see how they could have missed the significance of His *question regarding provision*.

"Jesus said to them, 'Children, do you have any fish?' They answered him, 'No'" (John 21:5 ESV).

I would think that this question not only reminded them of their initial calling, but also the Provider and His provision. I don't see how the fish and bread would not have reminded them of the feeding of the five thousand and of the four thousand. Jesus had tried to drive home the lesson of His provision for those who serve Him repeatedly. In fact, on one occasion He even chided them for not getting the simple truth that He would be their provision.

> Now they had forgotten to bring bread, and they had only one loaf with them in the boat. (Mark 8:14 ESV)
>
> And he said to them, "Do you not yet understand?" (Mark 8:21 ESV)
>
> But Jesus, aware of this, said, "O you of little faith, why are you discussing among yourselves the fact that you have no bread?
>
> Do you not yet perceive? Do you not remember the five loaves for the five thousand, and how many baskets you gathered?
>
> Or the seven loaves for the four thousand, and how many baskets you gathered?
>
> How is it that you fail to understand that I did not speak about bread? Beware of the leaven of the Pharisees and Sadducees." (Matt. 16:8–11 ESV)

So this first question seems to point to a wonderful promise regarding *provision* as these men are about to embark on such a challenging mission: *He will meet your needs if you will just be with Him!* They had Jesus—they had enough!

"Jesus said to them, I am the bread of life; whoever comes to me shall not hunger, and whoever believes in me shall never thirst" (John 6:35 ESV).

This breakfast also involved *questions regarding passion and purpose.*

> When they had finished breakfast, Jesus said to Simon Peter, "Simon, son of John, do you love me more than these?" He said to him, "Yes, Lord; you know that I love you." He said to him, "Feed my lambs."
>
> He said to him a second time, "Simon, son of John, do you love me?" He said to him, "Yes, Lord; you know that I love you." He said to him, "Tend my sheep."
>
> He said to him the third time, "Simon, son of John, do you love me?" Peter was grieved because he said to him the third time, "Do you love me?" and he said to him, "Lord, you know everything; you know that I love you." Jesus said to him, "Feed my sheep.
>
> Truly, truly, I say to you, when you were young, you used to dress yourself and walk wherever you wanted, but when you are old, you will stretch out your hands, and another will dress you and carry you where you do not want to go." (This he said to show by what kind of death he was to glorify God.) And after saying this, he said to him, "Follow me." (John 21:15–19 ESV)

This passage can seem a little confusing while reading it in the English text. It is much clearer in the Greek. In fact,

> the meaning of this section hinges upon the usage of two synonyms for love. In terms of interpretation, when two synonyms are placed in close proximity in context, a difference in meaning, however slight, is emphasized. When Jesus asked Peter if he loved Him, he used a word for love that signified total commitment. Peter responded with a word for love that signified his love for Jesus, but not necessarily his total commitment.[67]

The two words being used for "love" are *agape*—the word for total commitment, and *phileo*—the word for love for Jesus, but not necessarily his total commitment. I call this one *flawed love*.

I agree with many others who see this threefold question as corresponding to Peter's threefold denial. Peter loved Jesus, but he was no longer full of pride. He had been disobedient and denied the Savior in the past. He had made promises that he could not keep. He was reluctant to do that again.

The first question has the exchange of "do you truly love (*agape*) me? Yes, Lord, you know that I love (phileo) you." This question about *more than these* probably refers to the fish (v. 11) representing Peter's profession as a fisherman. It seems that it is possible, maybe likely, that it was a profession he was resuming at the beginning of this chapter. But Jesus had called him to leave all this and fish for men. His *purpose in ministry* is evoked by Jesus's "feed *my* lambs."

The second question moves away from the fish and focuses on *Peter's passion* for Jesus in a compelling way. "Simon, son of John, do you *truly* love (*agape*) me? Yes, Lord, you know that I love (*phileo*) you." Purpose in ministry is again pressed by Jesus "take care of my sheep."

When the question was asked a third time, which surely moved Peter into memories of his most vehement denial, it hurt Peter deeply. Not only the memory hurt him, but the change of Jesus' wording hurt him deeply. This time the exchange was, "Simon, son of John, do you love (phileo) me?" It must have broken Peter's heart to hear, "Do you even love me with a flawed love?"

Peter appeals to the Lord's very experiential knowledge of him and said, "Lord, you know that I truly love you even though my love is a flawed love." It must have been encouraging to again hear Jesus affirm Peter's usefulness for ministry. It was as if He was saying, "I can use a man with honest, flawed love—feed my sheep." This threefold emphasis on feeding and nourishing the sheep reinforces the primary duty of the messenger of Jesus Christ, which is to teach the Word of God (2 Tim. 4:2).

So this is an examination of the *passion* of a man who had made promises he could not keep. The good news is that it ends with this affirmation that Jesus can use a man with *flawed love.*

Interestingly, this breakfast also involved *a question regarding perspective.*

Jesus said to him, "If it is my will that he remain until I come, what is that to you? You follow me!" (John 21:22 ESV).

In 2008, I prepared a little talk to give to a team of people I was leading on a mission trip to Thailand. The talk was entitled *The Battle with Ourselves—a Look at the Jesus Followers*. It came from four passages regarding the disciples. The last one was this passage. I think that the disciples had some evident struggles as they followed Jesus and that we often struggle in the same ways as they did. Here are four that I noted:

- We often have our agenda—not God's.

> And he began to teach them that the Son of Man must suffer many things and be rejected by the elders and the chief priests and the scribes and be killed, and after three days rise again.
>
> And he said this plainly. And Peter took him aside and began to rebuke him.
>
> But turning and seeing his disciples, he rebuked Peter and said, "Get behind me, Satan! For you are not setting your mind on the things of God, but on the things of man." (Mark 8:31–33 ESV)

- We often want to be first—not last.

> They went on from there and passed through Galilee. And he did not want anyone to know, for he was teaching his disciples, saying to them, "The Son of Man is going to be delivered into the hands of men, and they will kill him.

And when he is killed, after three days he will rise."

But they did not understand the saying, and were afraid to ask him.

And they came to Capernaum. And when he was in the house he asked them, "What were you discussing on the way?"

But they kept silent, for on the way they had argued with one another about who was the greatest.

And he sat down and called the twelve. And he said to them, "If anyone would be first, he must be last of all and servant of all." (Mark 9:30–35 ESV)

- We often want the glory—not the cross.

And they were on the road, going up to Jerusalem, and Jesus was walking ahead of them. And they were amazed, and those who followed were afraid. And taking the twelve again, he began to tell them what was to happen to him, saying, "See, we are going up to Jerusalem, and the Son of Man will be delivered over to the chief priests and the scribes, and they will condemn him to death and deliver him over to the Gentiles.

And they will mock him and spit on him, and flog him and kill him. And after three days he will rise."

And James and John, the sons of Zebedee, came up to him and said to him, "Teacher, we want you to do for us whatever we ask of you."

And he said to them, "What do you want me to do for you?"

> And they said to him, "Grant us to sit, one at your right hand and one at your left, in your glory."
>
> Jesus said to them, "You do not know what you are asking. Are you able to drink the cup that I drink, or to be baptized with the baptism with which I am baptized?"
>
> And they said to him, "We are able." And Jesus said to them, "The cup that I drink you will drink, and with the baptism with which I am baptized, you will be baptized, but to sit at my right hand or at my left is not mine to grant, but it is for those for whom it has been prepared."
>
> And when the ten heard it, they began to be indignant at James and John.
>
> And Jesus called them to him and said to them, "You know that those who are considered rulers of the Gentiles lord it over them, and their great ones exercise authority over them.
>
> But it shall not be so among you. But whoever would be great among you must be your servant, and whoever would be first among you must be slave of all.
>
> For even the Son of Man came not to be served but to serve, and to give his life as a ransom for many." (Mark 10:32–45 ESV)

- We often examine others—not ourselves.

This last one occurred on this day when Peter had breakfast with Jesus.

"(This he said to show by what kind of death he was to glorify God.) And after saying this he said to him, 'Follow me'" (John 21:19–22 ESV).

Peter turned and saw the disciple whom Jesus loved following them, the one who also had leaned back against

> him during the supper and had said, "Lord, who is it that is going to betray you?"
>
> When Peter saw him, he said to Jesus, "Lord, what about this man?"
>
> Jesus said to him, "If it is my will that he remain until I come, what is that to you? You follow me!"
>
> This last one occurred on the day that Peter had breakfast with Jesus. After indicating the kind of death that Peter would one day experience, Jesus issued a very simple and direct command: "Follow me!"

But Peter couldn't just keep his eyes on his own business. He wanted to know about John and what Jesus had planned for John. I fear that we are so often like Peter here. We have a plan for the will of God for others. We want to tell Jesus how life should go for others, but we struggle with keeping our attention focused on our own lives and living out the plan of God for us.

This last "follow me" here is so instructive. It too is a present active imperative and the idea is that Jesus is commanding Peter to continually be concerned with his own obedience in following Him!

What a breakfast this was! As Peter was about to be released to his mission of making disciples, Jesus was kind enough to remind him that his needs would be met, that the Lord could use him even though his love was flawed, and that he must keep his attention on his own obedience to follow and let Jesus deal with the life and obedience of others.

The day I had breakfast with Jesus.

15

The Day I Stood up to Lead

Acts 1:12–26

The next encounter we are given regarding Peter's adventure with Jesus is in the book of Acts, and it is after the ascension of Jesus. It is the day that Peter *stood up to lead.*

I don't know of any group, organization, or family that has done well without someone stepping into the role of leadership. Yet leadership seems hard for many to define. *Webster's Dictionary* says this:

> Definition of leadership: there are lots of ideas of what leadership is.
>
> 1. The office or position of a leader.
> 2. The capacity to lead.
> 3. The act or an instance of leading. [68]

Now, wasn't that helpful!

While working on this passage, the *Daily Oklahoman* published an article by Ryan Aber on the struggling University of Oklahoma Women's Basketball team. It was an article on their struggle to find leadership. Head Coach Sherry Coale said, "But leading is—I don't know—it's such a hard thing to define. I'll have players say they want to be the guy. They really want to be the guy until they're the guy." [69]

I find this definition of leadership interesting: "The art of leadership…consists in consolidating the attention of the people against a single adversary and taking care that nothing will split up that attention."[70]

You know who said that? It was one of the most despicable leaders of history—Adolf Hitler!

For me personally, my favorite definition of leadership is also the simplest: *Leadership is influence.*

In this passage, we see just that. We see Peter lead by influencing the early followers of Jesus in their first decisions after Jesus had ascended to the Father.

I can only imagine this moment in history as the followers of Jesus (about a hundred and twenty in number—1:15) gathered in an upstairs room. The apostles (and other believers) are facing the monumental task of bearing witness to Jerusalem, Judea/Samaria, and the ends of the earth, and they are a man down because of Judas's betrayal.

As they await the baptism of the Spirit, there is much to prepare for. Someone will need to lead. It is at that time that "Peter stood up among the believers" (1:15) and led them to make a *choice.*

It was a choice *based upon the Scripture.*

> "Brothers, the Scripture had to be fulfilled, which the Holy Spirit spoke beforehand by the mouth of David concerning Judas, who became a guide to those who arrested Jesus.
>
> For he was numbered among us and was allotted his share in this ministry."
>
> (Now this man acquired a field with the reward of his wickedness, and falling headlong he burst open in the middle and all his bowels gushed out.
>
> And it became known to all the inhabitants of Jerusalem, so that the field was called in their own language Akeldama, that is, Field of Blood.)

> "For it is written in the Book of Psalms, 'May his camp become desolate, and let there be no one to dwell in it'; and 'Let another take his office.'" (Acts 1:16–20 ESV)

It is hard to remember that these men may well have loved Judas. They had spent three years with him. They didn't suspect him. They were very likely hurt by what he did and felt betrayed. He had been *numbered among them and had shared ministry with them.* Therefore, his initial statements may have been very comforting to them. Judas' acts and defection had been a part of God's purpose. Judas' replacement was also God's purpose.

Verse 20 is a quotation of Psalm 69:25 and Psalm 109:8. Peter had a clear confidence in the inspiration of Scripture. He based his leadership on the Scripture. He believed that the Scripture clearly was directing them to seek out a replacement for Judas. The Greek text (and some English translations) uses the word *dei*—"it is necessary" (used in vv. 16, 21). So the choice was based on Scripture, and it was mandated.

It was also a choice *based upon principle.* Before we talk about these principles, we probably need to talk about the biblical view of an *apostle*. I like the way that W. A. Criswell put it:

> The term "apostle" (Apostolos, Greek) is literally "one sent with a message." In its broadest sense, "apostle" denotes a missionary. In its narrowest sense, the word is assigned to the Twelve whom Jesus chose to be a part of His inner circle (cf. Luke 6:13). An apostle had to be baptized by John the Baptist and had to be a witness of the resurrection (v. 22). The zeal for filling the vacancy created by the death of Judas with someone who had the proper apostolic qualifications emphasizes two factors: (1) the awe with which they viewed apostleship and (2) the anticipation of great work which would require a full quota

> of officials. The qualifications (vv. 21ff) required that the vacancy be filled with someone who had been among the disciples with Jesus (v. 21), with special reference to his being a witness of the resurrection (v. 22). All of Christ's appearances were to believers only, except in the case of Paul at the time of his conversion. Apostles comprise a major portion of the foundation upon which the Christian ministry rests. The total foundation includes "apostles and prophets" (Eph. 2:20).[71]

It is interesting that as I examined the New Testament, I only found these listed apostles (out of a qualified possibility of probably less than six hundred—1 Corinthians 15:5–8—and since the only named apostles are men, that number is probably smaller):

- The Twelve
- Matthias
- Barnabas (Acts 14:14)
- James (the brother of Jesus, Gal. 1:19)
- Jesus (Heb. 3:1)
- Paul

So the *principles* involved in the successor's selection were that he had *participated in Jesus' earthly ministry* (v. 21–22—"went in and out among us") and that he had *seen the resurrected Christ* (v. 22—"must become with us a witness to his resurrection"). The resurrection of Jesus would be central to the proclamation of the apostles, so he had to have seen the resurrected Christ.

Finally, I love that this was a choice *based upon dependency.*

> "And they put forward two, Joseph called Barsabbas, who was also called Justus, and Matthias" (Acts 1:23–26 ESV).

> *And they prayed* and said, "You, Lord, who know the hearts of all, show which one of these two you have chosen to take the place in this ministry and apostleship from which Judas turned aside to go to his own place."
>
> *And they cast lots* for them, and the lot fell on Matthias, and he was numbered with the eleven apostles.

Their dependency was expressed in two ways. It was a dependency expressed in *supplication* (v. 24). They prayed for God's guidance. Everything began with prayer. "That prayer shows what we should be looking for most in a leader: 'Lord, you know everyone's heart. Show us which of these two you have chosen' (v. 24). The believers had found two people with suitable external qualifications, but those would be useless if the person's heart was not right. Only God knows the hearts of people unerringly, so they ask his help... Christian ministry is essentially spiritual in nature, and external qualifications are useless if a person's heart is not right with God."[72] We must pray. It is critical as we choose leaders. "If the apostles, who had been relatively close to these two candidates for at least two or three years needed this divine special guidance regarding the heart of the person, how much do we when we make a selection."[73]

I love what E. M. Bounds said of those who have effective spiritual leadership:

"They are not leaders because of brilliancy...but because, by the power of prayer, they could command the power of God."[74]

If Jesus spent the night in prayer before choosing his men (Luke 6:12–13) and the early church gave emphasis to prayer before choosing a leader, surely, we too should pray!

It was also a dependency embracing God's *sovereignty* (v. 26). They cast lots! I find the words of John MacArthur extremely helpful: "Casting the lots was a common OT method of determining God's will (cf. Lev. 16:8–10, Josh. 7:14, Prov. 18:18). This is the last biblical mention of lots—the coming of the Spirit made them unnecessary."[75]

Ajith Fernando is also helpful.

> According to the biblical usage, lots seem to have been used only when the decision was important and where wisdom or biblical injunctions did not give sufficient guidance. One of the advantages of the casting of lots was the impartiality of the choice...the only other time it appears in the New Testament is the soldiers casting lots for Jesus' garments (Matt. 27:35).[76]

They were looking for divine guidance. They wanted the choice to be sovereignly determined!

I believe that another comment from Fernando is especially important. "There is...no exegetical support in any New Testament text for the idea that the choice of Matthias to replace Judas was a mistake, and that Paul was God's man for the filling of the gap. Matthias's not being mentioned again in Acts is shared with eight other apostles!"[77]

Almost all who are reading this are leading someone! Some are business leaders. Some are influential students. Some are homeschooling parents, who are shaping the lives of future leaders. The day may be coming when the Living God asks you to stand up! He may soon call you to influence those you lead in a greater way. When that happens, please do it this way! Do it based upon the Scripture. Do it based upon clear biblical principles—that will include integrity and ethics. And do it with an absolute dependence on the Living God, who must help you to do it well!

There is so much to learn here about dealing with defection. Here we have the greatest leader that has ever walked this planet—the Lord Jesus. He was betrayed by one of His hand-picked followers. According to Acts 1:19, the outcome of Judas' life and betrayal was known to "all the inhabitants of Jerusalem." How humiliating!

Can you imagine the language of the first century regarding this? "That Jesus, He couldn't even pick twelve!"

I believe the early followers of Jesus were also deeply hurt by Judas's defection, but their deep sense of community and confidence in the sovereignty of God allowed them to move forward.

Paul was also deeply hurt by defection and disloyalty and that hurt continued right up to the end of his life (2 Tim. 4). But clearly, his story is one of continuing to open up his life to others and develop and engage them in ministry. I once did a study of the New Testament and counted the number of people that Paul mentioned by name, and it was astounding! And many of those he referred to as co-laborers in ministry.

It is this last truth that most moves me regarding this story. I wish someone had addressed this topic with me long ago. One of my greatest regrets over the last twenty years is in this area. I got hurt years ago by defection and because I didn't want to get hurt again, I quit personally investing in others in the way I had before. I will forever regret those lost opportunities. Dear reader, heed the testimony of the early church and Peter. Trust God's sovereign purpose. Don't let the defection of one stop you from embracing others in the pursuit of making disciples!

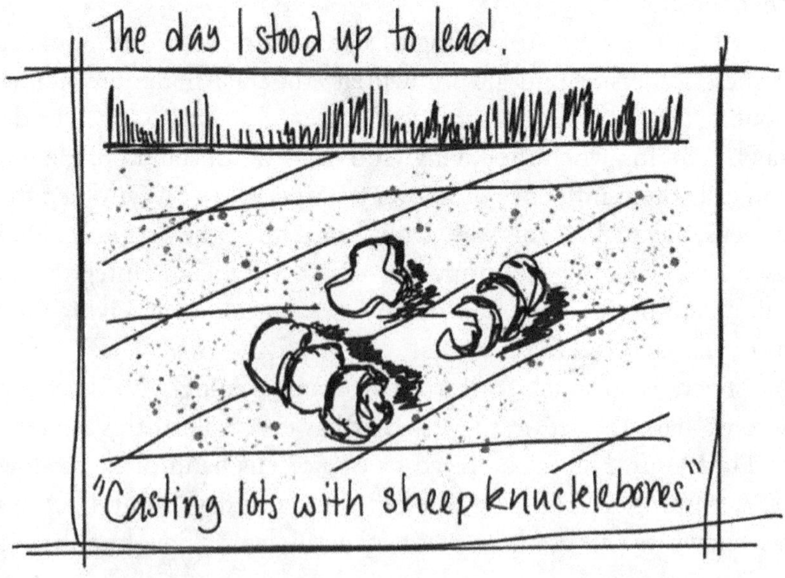

16

The Day I Stood up to Bear Witness

Acts 2:14–41

Peter and the other disciples had been waiting for a *day* (or event) that Jesus had promised that the Father would give them *a gift* (1:4). That gift would empower them, and they would then commence their assignment of being *witnesses* to the world!

"But you will receive power when the Holy Spirit has come upon you, and you will be my witnesses in Jerusalem and in all Judea and Samaria, and to the end of the earth" (Acts 1:8 ESV).

The *day* finally came on the day of Pentecost as God had assembled Jews from every nation under heaven (2:5) that they might hear a witness about the Lord Jesus.

"This Jesus God raised up, and of that we all are witnesses" (Acts 2:32 ESV).

As they began to bear witness in known languages, it caused a variety of responses of those gathered there (2:12–13). It was in the midst of this environment that *Peter stood up…raised his voice* and began to bear witness (1:14).

Bearing witness is an interesting thing. Maybe you heard the story about a prosecuting attorney from a small Texas town, who called his first witness to the stand in a trial. She was a grandmotherly type, and he asked her, "Mrs. Jones, do you know me?"

She said, "I do know you, Mr. Williams. I've known you since you were a young boy. And to be honest, you have been a big disappointment. You lie, you cheat on your wife, and manipulate people and talk about them behind their backs. You think you are some big shot on the rise, but you don't have the brains to realize you are nothing more than a two-bit paper pusher. Yes, sir, I know you!"

The lawyer was stunned. Not knowing what else to do, he pointed across the room and asked, "Mrs. Williams, do you know the defense attorney?"

She replied, "Yes I do. I've known Mr. Bradley since he was a youngster, as well. In fact, I used to babysit him for his parents. He, too, has been a real disappointment. He is lazy, bigoted, and has a drinking problem. The man can't form or hold a decent relationship with anyone, and his law practice is one of the shoddiest in the entire state. Yes, sir, I know him too."

The crowd began to murmur and the noise level in the courtroom rose to an unacceptable level with all the people responding to what had just been said. The sound of the judge's gavel rang through the courtroom, and the judge motioned for both attorneys to approach the bench. When they were in front of the judge, he whispered to them in a very quiet voice, "If either of you asks her if she knows me, I'll have you thrown in jail for contempt!"

In a courtroom setting, she was what we might call a very forthcoming witness!

Unfortunately, Christ-followers, who have the greatest news to share are not always so forthcoming. I read the story of a Christian who prayed, "Lord, if you want me to witness to someone today, please give me a sign to show me who it is."

That very day he found himself on a nearly empty bus when a big, burly man sat next to him. The timid believer anxiously waited for his stop so he could exit the bus. However, before he could get off, the big burly guy next to him burst into tears and began to weep. This big but contrite man then cried out with a loud voice, "I'm a lost sinner, and I need the Lord. Won't somebody tell me how to be saved?" He turned to this Christian gentleman and pleaded, "Can you show me how to find the Lord?"

The believer immediately bowed his head and prayed, "Lord, is this a sign?"

I'm not sure about that guy! But I admire those who *stand up and bear witness*! In November of 2018, I became aware of one of those people—a twenty-year-old student senator at the University of California Berkeley named Isabella Chow.

Isabella experienced intense opposition for voicing her Christian beliefs on sexual identity and gender. There were demands that she resign from the Senate or face recall. There were fears that funding for Christian groups on campus would be threatened. A piano recital where she was supposed to play was cancelled because professors said, "You can't perform when we are all afraid of protestors showing up at the door." At one protest, people yelled at her for three hours, swearing and demanding that she resign.

Her offense? Chow chose *to not vote* on October 31, on a measure decrying consideration by the Trump administration of a legal definition that says a person's gender is what his or her sex was at birth. She was the only one of twenty senators to abstain on the measure, which also backed organizations that promote the LGBT agenda.

In a statement on Facebook explaining why she abstained, Chow first said discrimination "is never, ever okay." But she said, "Where this bill crosses the line for me is that I am asked to promote a choice of identities that I do not agree with to be right or best for an individual, and to promote certain organizations that uphold values contrary to those of my community."[78]

I admire that young lady. I also admire Peter as he stands up on this day and bears witness to the Lord Jesus. He begins his speech by answering a real question being asked by the audience about the languages they were hearing—"What does this mean?"

Here is his answer:

This was a day of promise (vv. 14–21). Peter first addressed Joel 2:28–32a. He said that this was a *promised day*: *this is what was spo-*

ken! It is also a reference to Isaiah 44:3 and Ezekiel 39:29. I appreciate how Ajith Fernando puts it:

> A key to understanding Peter's speech is to grasp the fact that he was attempting to show the Jews from Scripture and from events that had taken place (especially the resurrection) that the gospel of Christ has been validated and accredited as true. He attempted to show incontrovertible evidence.[79]

It was a promised day to Israel, but it was also *a day of promise* because God was going to *pour out His Spirit on all people* (see verses 17, 21, 39)!

Peter makes it clear that this was also *a day about a person* (vv. 22–36).

"And it shall come to pass that everyone who calls upon the name of the Lord shall be saved" (Acts 2:21 ESV).

This is a quotation of Joel 2:32a, which says, "And everyone who calls on the name of the Lord will be saved."

A logical question among that first century audience would have been "What is the name of the Lord that we are to call on?"

Peter's answer is that the name is *Jesus* (v. 22)! He even uses a rare word—*apodeiknumi*—which means "to exhibit, show forth, display, attest, demonstrate something is true, to prove," to say that God evidenced that *this was a day about a person*. In fact, this section is bracketed by the answer of *Jesus* (see v. 36)!

A second question would be, "How did God evidence it?" He *evidenced it by the miraculous.*

"Men of Israel, hear these words: Jesus of Nazareth, a man attested to you by God with mighty works and wonders and signs that God did through him in your midst, as you yourselves know" (Acts 2:22 ESV).

I love those last four words! They knew. The text is silent regarding their objections because they did indeed know!

He also *evidenced it by the crucifixion.*

"This Jesus, delivered up according to the definite plan and foreknowledge of God, you crucified and killed by the hands of lawless men" (Acts 2:23 ESV).

Thirdly, He *evidenced it by the resurrection* (Acts 2:23–32). Peter referenced Psalm 16:8–11. In doing so, he said that the One who will not be abandoned to the grave and will not see decay is not David but Jesus (see v. 31)!

"God raised him up, loosing the pangs of death, because it was not possible for him to be held by it" (Acts 2:24 ESV).

And finally, He *evidenced it by the ascension.*

"Being therefore exalted at the right hand of God, and having received from the Father the promise of the Holy Spirit, he has poured out this that you yourselves are seeing and hearing" (Acts 2:33 ESV).

Jesus' exaltation made it possible for him to send the promised Holy Spirit (see also John 16:7), whose life and ministry is poured out on all the church.

"For the promise is for you and for your children and for all who are far off, everyone whom the Lord our God calls to himself" (Acts 2:39 ESV).

This was not just a day of promise and a day about a person, it was also *a day that was piercing and persuasive.*

"Now when they heard this they were cut to the heart, and said to Peter and the rest of the apostles, 'Brothers, what shall we do?'" (Acts 2:37–40 ESV).

> And Peter said to them, "Repent and be baptized every one of you in the name of Jesus Christ for the forgiveness of your sins, and you will receive the gift of the Holy Spirit.
>
> For the promise is for you and for your children and for all who are far off, everyone whom the Lord our God calls to himself."
>
> And with many other words he bore witness and continued to exhort them, saying, "Save yourselves from this crooked generation."

Peter had become very personal when he said, "This Jesus, whom *you* crucified." This pierced or cut them to the heart and led to the question of "what shall we do?" Peter became very persuasive as he encouraged them to repent and be baptized and be saved. In fact, the words "save yourselves" is an aorist passive imperative. It should be translated "be saved."

I distinctly remember what it is like to be "cut to the heart." It was a Saturday night. I had taken the lady who would become my wife on a date. I dropped her off at her parents' home. I drove the short distance to my parents' home. As I went inside, an almost two-year period of conviction culminated in my life. The Holy Spirit of God cut me to the heart in such a way that it was time to deal with my sin problem. He graciously drew me to the Savior on that night!

Finally, and gloriously, this was *a day for praise.*

> "So those who received his word were baptized, and there were added that day about three thousand souls." (Acts 2:41 ESV)

What a mighty work of the Spirit—about three thousand souls saved! The Church was off and running with a great harvest of souls on the day that the Spirit was poured out. This glorious work was also a promise of Jesus fulfilled.

"Truly, truly, I say to you, whoever believes in me will also do the works that I do; and greater works than these will he do, because I am going to the Father" (John 14:12 ESV).

At the conclusion of Jesus' ministry there were only about 120 believers (Acts 1:15). Now, after the outpouring of the Spirit, His followers were enabled to *greater works* and the Church grew by about three thousand in one day!

"This Jesus God raised up, and of that we all are witnesses" (Acts 2:32 ESV).

What an amazing *witness* Peter was on this day for the Lord Jesus. I think that there are a number of things that we can learn from him regarding our own witness.

The first thing is, in our witness, *let us be courageous.* We cannot allow ourselves to forget that *Peter stood up* in the very Jerusalem where His Lord had been crucified. It was also the very city, among the very people where he had been full of fear and denied His Lord. Now, the fullness of the Spirit produced *courage*! Truthfully, this principle has caused me concern. It has caused me to contemplate. If the fullness of the Spirit produces confidence, does a lack of confidence indicate a lack of the fullness of the Spirit?

Second, in our witness, *let us be focused.* Peter could have spent his time focused on the person and ministry of the Spirit. Or he could have focused on the phenomena observed that day. Instead, he focused on Jesus! The first evangelistic sermon of the New Testament church focused on Christ—may we do the same!

Lastly, in our witness, *let us be persuasive.* Peter sure was. By the fullness of the Spirit, may we be *persuasive* enough to point out sin (2:23). By the fullness of the Spirit, may we be *persuasive* enough to kindly call people to repentance (2:38). By the fullness of the Spirit, may we be *persuasive* enough to warn people of judgment to come (2:40). By the fullness of the Spirit, may we be *persuasive* enough to call for decision (2:40).

During my time working on this *day* in Peter's life, I attended the funeral of a fellow Christ follower I had served the Lord with several decades earlier. As I walked into the chapel, I looked into the pastor's holding room I had been in many times and there sat my friend, Pastor Ruffin Snow.

During the memorial, Ruffin told how Vic had made it very clear to him what songs he wanted sung and the scope of the message he wanted delivered. An important part of that message was that he wanted people to hear the witness of the Gospel of the Lord Jesus. Ruffin did that and then concluded with a story about himself and fellow pastor Tom Elliff arriving quickly on the scene of the bombing of the Murrow Federal Building in downtown Oklahoma City on April 19, 1995.

They were quickly credentialed as counselors and began the long and arduous endeavor to assist the families who had lost loved ones or those still waiting to learn the fate of the their loved one.

Ruffin told of his encounter with one woman, a Christ follower, whose husband had perished in the bombing. She told him how people had shared Jesus with her husband, and he had rejected Christ. She told him how she had loved him and shared Jesus with him, but he had rejected Christ. He said she asked him one question that had stuck with him all these years. The question was, "How much time does a person need to make that decision (to receive Christ)?"

She was wanting to know if there was any possibility that as those floors collapsed on her husband, would there have been time for him to give his life to Christ if he had chosen to in that instant?

Ruffin said that he drove away from those hours of trying to help people angry. He is not a man that I have ever seen angry, so that caught my attention. He said that he was angry at that man. His rejection of Christ had cost him a Christ-less eternity, and it had broken the heart of those who loved him. And then, with great courage, focus, and persuasion, Ruffin bore witness of the One who is the way, the truth, and the life and kindly urged all in attendance to truly know Him.

By the fullness of God's Spirit, may we do the same!

17

The Day I Encountered a Panhandler

Acts 3:1–4:22

Here is how the dictionary defines what a *panhandler* does: *"to accost passers-by on the street and beg from them."*

As I write this chapter the United States unemployment rate is at an historic low. But in my city, there are more and more *panhandlers* everywhere including in some rural areas. Some of them have really creative signs. While Googling this, I came across two I really liked. One said, "Parents eaten by pigeons. Need money for BB gun!" My other favorite said, "My father was killed by ninjas. Need money for karate lessons!"

I have seen some news articles and television reports suggesting that panhandlers make a pretty healthy income. During my work on this chapter, I ran across a *New York Post* magazine showing a panhandler who boasted of making $200 an hour! In 2019, I saw a local news report suggesting that panhandlers in our city made an annual income in the low $30,000 range. Yet as I have attempted some research, the reality appears to be about $30 a day.

This is not a recent societal development. It was in existence in the first century as well. In this passage, we encounter just such a man. He had been crippled from birth (v. 2) and was now over forty years old (4:22)!

> "Now Peter and John were going up to the temple at the hour of prayer, the ninth hour." (Acts 3:1–5 ESV)
>
> And a man lame from birth was being carried, whom they laid daily at the gate of the temple that is called the Beautiful Gate to ask alms of those entering the temple.
>
> Seeing Peter and John about to go into the temple, he asked to receive alms.
>
> And Peter directed his gaze at him, as did John, and said, "Look at us."
>
> And he fixed his attention on them, expecting to receive something from them.
>
> "For the man on whom this sign of healing was performed was more than forty years old." (Acts 4:22 ESV)

It is this man that Peter encounters on this day and an incredible *event* occurs! Luke has just told his readers that the early church was marked by miraculous signs and wonders done by the apostles and now Peter is used by God to perform one as he takes the man's hand and *instantly* what had not worked in over four decades is healed and strengthened to the extent that he walked and leapt in his praise to God!

> "But Peter said, 'I have no silver and gold, but what I do have I give to you. In the name of Jesus Christ of Nazareth, rise up and walk!'" (Acts 3:6–10 ESV)
>
> And he took him by the right hand and raised him up, and immediately his feet and ankles were made strong.

> And leaping up, he stood and began to walk, and entered the temple with them, walking and leaping and praising God.
>
> And all the people saw him walking and praising God, and recognized him as the one who sat at the Beautiful Gate of the temple, asking for alms. And they were filled with wonder and amazement at what had happened to him.

Can you imagine being there that day? There were all kinds of responses of those present to the miraculous event. Luke notes the response of *the people* in two ways. The first is that verse 10 said that "all the people were filled with wonder and amazement." Now verse 11 says they were "utterly astounded." *Thambos* in verse 10 becomes *ekthambos* in verse 11 (the only time it is used in the New Testament). They were *out of their mind with amazement*!

"While he clung to Peter and John, all the people, utterly astounded, ran together to them in the portico called Solomon's Colonnade" (Acts 3:11 ESV).

The second thing he notes about the response of the people is that this became the platform upon which he presented the Gospel and that a number of them believed!

"But many of those who had heard the word believed, and the number of the men came to about five thousand" (Acts 4:4 ESV).

The response of others is not so positive. The reality is that a theme surfaces here that will recur throughout Acts—the rejection of the Messiah by the Jews—particularly their official leadership. We can note it in the response of *the priests, captain of the guard, and the Sadducees.*

> And as they were speaking to the people, the priests and the captain of the temple and the Sadducees came upon them, greatly annoyed because they were teaching the people and proclaiming in Jesus the resurrection from the dead.

> And they arrested them and put them in custody until the next day, for it was already evening. (Acts 4:1–3 ESV)

They were "greatly annoyed." The word here is *diapoveomai*. It is only used three times in the New Testament and two of the three are here in the book of Acts. It is used in Acts 16:18 to describe Paul's frustration with a demon possessed girl that continued to follow him.

"And this she kept doing for many days. Paul, having become greatly annoyed, turned and said to the spirit, 'I command you in the name of Jesus Christ to come out of her.' And it came out that very hour" (Acts 16:18 ESV).

It is also used in Mark 14:4 to describe the disgust of some over what they perceived as waste by the woman who poured perfume on the head of Jesus.

"There were some who said to themselves indignantly, 'Why was the ointment wasted like that?'" (Mark 14:4 ESV).

The word means "to be greatly disturbed, annoyed, or to be irked." They were ticked!

Then there is the response of *the rulers and elders*. We are told *what they saw*. They saw courage and boldness.

"Now when they saw the boldness of Peter and John" (Acts 4:13a ESV).

We are also told *what they noted*. Realizing that they were common, uneducated men, they were astonished by them. They recognized (NIV = "took note of") that the only explanation was that they had been with Jesus.

"And perceived that they were uneducated, common men, they were astonished. And they recognized that they had been with Jesus" (Acts 4:13b ESV).

Then we are told *what they considered*. They considered, "What shall we do with these men?" They could not deny the miracle, but they desperately wanted to stop the spread of the Gospel!

> But when they had commanded them to leave the council, they conferred with one

> another, saying, "What shall we do with these men? For that a notable sign has been performed through them is evident to all the inhabitants of Jerusalem, and we cannot deny it.
>
> But in order that it may spread no further among the people, let us warn them to speak no more to anyone in this name. (Acts 4:15–17 ESV)

Finally, we are told *what they commanded.* They commanded them not to speak or teach at all in the name of Jesus.

"So they called them and charged them not to speak or teach at all in the name of Jesus" (Acts 4:18 ESV).

This encounter with the *panhandler* has at least four truths of application for us. The first is that *practical assistance is often the springboard to the Gospel.* Meeting a practical need often opens the heart for the greater need of the Gospel. Jesus did this and so did his disciples. We should as well.

The second truth is that *practical assistance is not enough.* In this man's case, it was clearly not enough! Peter immediately moves from the question of *how* he was healed to *salvation is found in no one else* than Jesus. I like the comments of Ajith Fernando:

> While human aspirations and problems are dealt with and are often the launching pad for evangelism, ultimately what matters is what God has done in Jesus for human kind and how individuals respond to that…the apostles often started with questions people had. But they used those questions as stepping stones for presenting the foundational truths of the gospel, which are what ultimately matter…it started by dealing with a human need…this led to a miracle and then to a sermon…people usually come within the sound of the gospel in order to avail themselves of the power of God for personal needs.

> But they stay because they know Christianity is the truth.[80]

Fernando is also helpful in his quotation of the Earl of Shaftesbury (who was a great *social reformer* in Britain). Shaftesbury said, "All life is reduced to a transaction between the individual soul and the individual Savior, and, my faith is summed up in one word, and that is Jesus."[81]

While working on this chapter, I attended a funeral in Wewoka, Oklahoma. I drove through about three hours of driving rain, there and back, to attend. It was the funeral of a man on my dad's side of the family. It was important to my dad that I was there, so I went, even though I only knew a couple of those who attended.

The dead man's son told an intriguing story about his dad. His dad was a collector of keys. He had hundreds of keys on his key ring and he always carried them with him. That son said that as he walked out of the room where his dad died, he noticed that there lay his dad's keys. This ring that represented all of his dad's possessions was left. He didn't take anything with him! His eternity came down to what he had done with Jesus!

The third truth is that *God delights in using the ordinary for the extraordinary*. The language in 4:13 is interesting to me.

"Now when they saw the boldness of Peter and John, and perceived that they were uneducated, common men, they were astonished. And they recognized that they had been with Jesus" (Acts 4:13 ESV).

It says that they *perceived* (to understand, *katalambano*) that the disciples were *uneducated* (unlettered, illiterate, *agrammatos*, only used here in the New Testament) and *common* (unlearned, unskilled, *idiotes*, only used five times in the New Testament) men!

John MacArthur says it well:

> They were amazed that uneducated (in the rabbinical schools) and untrained men (not professional theologians; laymen) could argue so effectively from the Scriptures. That two

> Galilean fishermen powerfully and successfully argued their case before the elite Jewish supreme court was shocking, so that they were marveling. What triggered the Sanhedrin's recognition was the realization that the apostles were doing what Jesus did. Like the apostles, Jesus had boldly and fearlessly confronted the Jewish leaders with His authority and truth (cf. Matt. 7:28–29). He, too, had no formal rabbinic training (cf. John 7:15–16). Yet in His sure handling of the Old Testament Scriptures He had no equal (cf. John 7:46). Jesus had performed many miracles during His earthly ministry. Peter and John were on trial largely because of a miracle they had performed.[82]

You may consider yourself untrained and unskilled. You may consider yourself very common and ordinary. I have good news for you! Our God delights in using the ordinary for His extraordinary purpose to display His glory!

Finally, this story reminds us that *a disciple chooses obedience to God in spite of difficulty or danger.* There is such courage and boldness here! There is such Spirit-filled obedience!

I don't know the origin, but I love the statement that "courage is not the absence of fear, but rather the judgment that something else is more important than fear."

Again, MacArthur is helpful:

> Peter refused to compromise the gospel by deleting what would offend the Sanhedrin. He spoke courageously because he was devoted to the truth and entrusted the outcome to his Lord. That is an example for all persecuted believers to follow…ironically, the early believers had to be commanded to be quiet, while many modern ones have to be commanded to speak. This was an important crossroads in the history of the church.

> Had the apostles acquiesced to the Sanhedrin's demand, all subsequent church history would have been radically different. Everything hinged on their willingness to obey God at all costs—even their lives.[83]

It is interesting how Peter said it later in life: "Now who is there to harm you if you are zealous for what is good?" (1 Peter 3:13–15 ESV).

But even if you should suffer for righteousness' sake, you will be blessed. Have no fear of them, nor be troubled, but in your hearts honor Christ the Lord as holy, always being prepared to make a defense to anyone who asks you for a reason for the hope that is in you; yet do it with gentleness and respect.

So, dear reader, have the courage to obey no matter the cost. I hope this last story will encourage you to step into whatever the Lord calls you to. It appeared years ago in *Chicken Soup for the Soul.* [84] Someone wrote:

> Many years ago, when I worked as a volunteer at Stanford Hospital, I got to know a little girl named Liza who was suffering from a rare and serious disease. Her only chance of recovery appeared to be a blood transfusion from her five-year-old brother, who had miraculously survived the same disease and had developed the antibodies needed to combat the illness. The doctor explained the situation to her little brother and asked the boy if he would be willing to give his blood to the sister. I saw him hesitate for only a moment before taking a deep breath and saying, "Yes, I'll do it if it will save Liza."
>
> As the transfusion progressed, he lay in a bed next to his sister and smiled, as we all did, seeing the color returning to her cheeks. Then his face grew pale and his smile faded. He looked up

> at the doctor and asked with a trembling voice, "Will I start to die right away?"
>
> Being young, the boy had misunderstood the doctor; he thought he was going to have to give her all his blood.

But he courageously embraced the cost because of love for the one for whom he was risking it all. May our love for Christ cause us to courageously risk whatever we must risk that we might obey Him!

18

The Day I Stood against Deception

Acts 5:1–11

Around the time that I trusted Christ, I heard one of the greatest conversion stories that I have heard in my life. It was such a vivid story and an amazing radical transformation of a life! The story even became a book, which was very well received. Unfortunately, some years later it was discovered that the story was fabricated. It was a deception!

While I was working on a second bachelor's degree, I met a fellow student, a black man, from the state of Florida. Within a few years he became a national sensation because of his unique communication skills and his sensational testimony about growing up under a bridge as a homeless youth. His story ultimately caught the attention of a well-known religious personality who put his story on television including the young man's reunion in a hospital with his biological father. Unfortunately, an investigative reporter with the *Dallas Morning News* exposed the story as a fraud. It was a deception!

For years, the churches I served went to a particular camp in the summer for our students. It was a wonderful place where the Lord did a mighty work in many of our lives, students, and adults alike. One year we had the most phenomenal mission speaker I had ever heard. He told the story of his near martyrdom and then massive conversion of nearly an entire tribe. But a few years later, it was exposed for being untrue. It was a deception!

Here in Acts 5, we have a devastating deception in the life of the early church. It involved a couple named *Ananias and Sapphira*. Our guy Peter steps right into the middle of the whole affair.

We are first alerted to *the sell of their property*.

"But a man named Ananias, with his wife Sapphira, sold a piece of property, and with his wife's knowledge he kept back for himself some of the proceeds and brought only a part of it and laid it at the apostles' feet" (Acts 5:1–2 ESV).

The background of this event is better pointed to in the NIV: "*also* sold a piece of property." This had been an ongoing characteristic of the early church. We see it in Acts 2:44–45 and again in Acts 4:32–37. The later passage differs in that one of those who gave (Barnabas) was recognized by name. This must have caught the attention of Ananias and Sapphira and ignited a desire to be recognized on their part. Their story is presented as a contrast ("*but* a man named Ananias") to the preceding story of Barnabas.

There was a "spirit of sharing" in the early church! That is what makes the deception so disgusting as we consider *the sinister nature of their ploy*. We can see the ploy by comparing verse 2 and verse 8.

> And with his wife's knowledge he kept back for himself some of the proceeds and brought only a part of it and laid it at the apostles' feet. (Acts 5:2 ESV)

> And Peter said to her, "Tell me whether you sold the land for so much." And she said, "Yes, for so much." (Acts 5:8 ESV)

The issue was *not* the selling of the land. The issue was *not* whether or not to give the money. The issue was *not* whether they gave all the money. The issue was that they *lied*! "Kept back" (Gk. *nospohizo*) literally means "to pilfer, embezzle." The word appears again in the New Testament only in verse 3 and Titus 2:10 where it is translated "steal"!

And the ploy (lie) was seen as *sinister* in nature. Notice the language used here:

But Peter said, "Ananias, why has Satan filled your heart to lie to the Holy Spirit and to keep back for yourself part of the proceeds of the land?" (Acts 5:3–4 ESV).

While it remained unsold, did it not remain your own? And after it was sold, was it not at your disposal? Why is it that you have contrived this deed in your heart? You have not lied to man but to God."

- Satan filled your heart.
- Lie to the Holy Spirit.
- Contrived this deed.
- Lied…to God.
- Test the Spirit of the Lord.

This is seen by the Apostle Peter as absolutely *sinister in nature!* And he is apparently not alone!

"When Ananias heard these words, he fell down and breathed his last. And great fear came upon all who heard of it" (Acts 5:5–6 ESV).

The young men rose and wrapped him up and carried him out and buried him.

"But Peter said to her, 'How is it that you have agreed together to test the Spirit of the Lord? Behold, the feet of those who have buried your husband are at the door, and they will carry you out'" (Acts 5:9–10 ESV).

Immediately she fell down at his feet and breathed her last. When the young men came in, they found her dead, and they carried her out and buried her beside her husband.

God responds swiftly and severely in both the lives of Ananias and Sapphira! And it causes the whole church to respond in such a way that it expresses *the solemnity of their peril.*

Solemnity means "serious or awesome quality, gravity." Both verse 5 and verse 11 say that the seriousness or gravity of their deaths produced *great fear* upon the whole church and all who heard what had happened. Everyone saw that God had judged the couple for their *deception*. "This was a fear of displeasing God that comes from a knowledge of his holiness and the consequences of our sin."[85]

There are a least three warnings that apply to us as we contemplate this day in Peter's life. The first is that we should *beware the insidious lure of wanting to be recognized.* It is clear in the text that giving everything wasn't compelled. The thing that Satan filled their heart for was a desire to be recognized by the church. Ajith Fernando's comments are interesting:

> Demonization denotes the occurrence in the lives of Christians when Satan gets them so obsessed with an idea or course of action that they get carried away and are blinded to the consequences. That seems to be what is happening here.[86]

And of course, the root of wanting this kind of recognition is often pride. We would do well to remember the Lord's disgust with our pride.

"The fear of the Lord is hatred of evil. Pride and arrogance and the way of evil and perverted speech I hate" (Prov. 8:13 ESV).

We should also *beware the folly of trifling with God.* Though the Lord does not always respond in this way, we must take care to not sin against Him in such a way. Not only does this story urge us to beware, but so do countless others like Nadab and Abihu (Lev. 10), Uzzah (2 Samuel 6), and Achan (Joshua 7). Again, I appreciate the insight of Ajith Fernando:

> The LXX uses this word (nophizo) for Achan, who kept some of the booty from the spoils of war that had been devoted to God. There, as here, the sin met with a severe pun-

> ishment. The rarity of the word in the New Testament suggests that Luke deliberately drew on the language of the Old Testament.[87]

Finally, we should *beware the church that takes lightly the things of God.* This is the first of twenty-three times that the word *ekklesia* is used in Acts. Fernando's words are piercing:

> *Untruthfulness...hinders fellowship in the body...lying is a deadly cancer that can destroy the life of a body. When people are untrue, they cannot be genuine.*[88]

I don't know about you, but I am hesitant to be a part of a church that takes lightly the things of God where this kind of blatant deception can be fostered and my church, my family, and my life can be in the place where the blessing of God is withheld.

My dear wife has endured both her parents getting cancer and dying from it. On both occasions, she went with them for a scan to see where it was in their bodies. For example, her dad's cancer had started in his lungs, but by the time the scan was done, it lit up all over his body. Cancer was in his brain, his major organs, it was everywhere. From diagnosis to death was about six weeks.

I wonder if there was a scan for this kind of behavior in the modern church, and it was administered—would the Body light up?

I would like to conclude this chapter in Peter's life with the comments of the late Warren Wiersbe:

> Ananias means "God is gracious," but he learned that God is also holy; and Sapphira means 'beautiful,' but her heart was ugly with sin. They learned that God is gracious and beautiful, but He is also holy and hates sin! If God killed "religious deceivers" today, how many church members would be left?[89]

It is as if the writer of Hebrews had this story in mind when he wrote these words: "Therefore let us be grateful for receiving a kingdom that cannot be shaken, and thus let us offer to God acceptable worship, with reverence and awe, for our God is a consuming fire" (Heb. 12:28–29 ESV).

I once heard Charles Swindoll say something that I have never gotten over: "*God is not safe*!" Beware taking His holiness for granted!

19

The Day I Dealt with the Sorcerer

Acts 8:9–25

This part of Peter's story is also an important part in the history of the church. The church's clear mission was to take the gospel to the whole world (Acts 1:8), and by and large, the church had yet to leave Jerusalem. But the events of chapters 6 and 7 would change all of that.

> Stephen's ministry prepared the church theologically by freeing Christianity from the Jerusalem temple. His death and the persecution that followed propelled witnessing Christians out of Jerusalem. The present chapter contains two key steps in this direction—the conversion of Samaritans and of an Ethiopian.[90]

That is the language of the beginning of the eighth chapter:

> And Saul approved of his execution. And there arose on that day a great persecution against the church in Jerusalem, and they were all scattered throughout the regions of Judea and Samaria, except the apostles. (Acts 8:1 ESV)

> Now those who were scattered went about preaching the word. (Acts 8:4 ESV)

So we must remember that this scene in Peter's life occurs among the Samaritans. They are

> descendants of Jews of the northern kingdom who intermarried with foreigners. They were not regarded as Gentiles by the Jews, but as part of 'the lost sheep of the house of Israel.' Their religion was based on the Pentateuch, though their Pentateuch was different in a few places to the one we are familiar with. They were awaiting a future deliverer in keeping with the promise of Deuteronomy 18:15–19 about the coming of a prophet like Moses (cf. the Samaritan woman in John 4, who referred to the hope of the coming Messiah, John 4:25). Phillip seems to have built on this hope when he preached the Messiah there. It was a bold step he took since bad feelings existed between Jews and Samaritans.[91]

Phillip's ministry caught the attention of the crowds (8:6) and brought joy to the city of Samaria (8:8). It even caught the attention of the most influential and significant men of the city (8:10). The language in verse 10 clearly identifies *the man's popularity*. Yet when he is introduced it is with an element of foreboding:

> *But* there was a man named Simon, who had previously practiced magic in the city and amazed the people of Samaria, saying that he himself was somebody great.
>
> They all paid attention to him, from the least to the greatest, saying, "This man is the power of God that is called Great."

> And they paid attention to him because for a long time he had amazed them with his magic. (Acts 8:9–11 ESV)

The NKJV here called him "a sorcerer" or wizard. Sorcery is "magic which originally referred to the practices of the Medo-Persians: a mixture of science and superstition, including astrology, divination, and the occult (Deut. 18:9–12; Rev. 9:21)."[92] I also find W. A. Criswell helpful here. He said,

> This is Christianity's first sharp confrontation with gross superstition and cultism, which were widespread in the first century AD. Moses had listed no fewer than ten 'abominations' of the nations, particularly of Canaan. He strongly warned the Israelites just before their crossing the Jordan into the Promised Land (Deut. 18:9–14). Sorcery is literally 'magic arts' from *mageuo* (Gk.), the root for the English word 'magic.' Moses warned the Israelites that Canaan would be filled with the practitioners of Wizardry, necromancy, and divination, etc. He then indicated to the chosen people that God was instituting prophecy precisely to teach and to warn the Israelites about such things. Sorcery and its like were wholly unacceptable to the God of Israel (cf. Lev. 20:6, 27; Deut. 17:2–5). Moses indicated that the prophets, which God was going to send, apparently beginning with Joshua, would teach and condition the people for resisting such practices…in the encounter of Christianity with the cultural milieu of Samaria, one of the first stubborn resisters to the gospel was this man Simon.[93]

Simon is called Simon Magus in postapostolic writings—Magus being a word given for

> people who practice sorcery. According to these writings he led many people astray.[94]

We not only see the man's popularity, but we also learn of *the man's profession* of faith.

> But when they believed Philip as he preached good news about the kingdom of God and the name of Jesus Christ, they were baptized, both men and women.
>
> Even Simon himself believed, and after being baptized he continued with Philip. And seeing signs and great miracles performed, he was amazed. (Acts 8:12–13 ESV)

Of course, the question here is about whether or not Simon was truly converted. As someone has rightly stated—there is a great difference between *profession* and *possession*! He has made a profession of faith. He has been baptized. But I am going to argue that Simon was *not* truly converted.

I realize that someone might say, "But wait a minute. The text says he *believed.* Indeed, it does. But I can think of at least three examples in the New Testament where it says that there is belief but no conversion. The first is James 2:19: 'You believe that God is one; you do well. Even the demons believe—and shudder!'" (ESV).

There is clear mental assent here by the demons. They acknowledge who He is and clearly know that He is exactly whom the Scripture declares Him to be, but there is no surrender to His Lordship or affection for Him!

A second example is in John 2.

> Now when he was in Jerusalem at the Passover Feast, many believed in his name when they saw the signs that he was doing.

> But Jesus on his part did not entrust himself to them, because he knew all people and needed no one to bear witness about man, for he himself knew what was in man. (John 2:23–25 ESV)

They assented to who He was, but they did not yield their lives to Him and Jesus "did not entrust himself to them" because He knew them, and He knew their profession was false.

This is the third example in the New Testament, and I believe that the text clearly evidences the truth concerning Simon's profession, and we will examine that in a few moments.

It is at this point of the story that our guy Peter arrives on the scene having been sent to investigate by the apostles. This is an incredibly significant passage. Thank God they sent to them Peter and John! Samaritans were considered by full-blooded Jews to be half-breeds. They weren't considered Gentiles. They were counted as "the lost sheep of Israel." There was an incredible animosity and hatred between the Jews and the Samaritans. Remember that Jesus encounters a Samaritan woman at the well in John 4? Remember also that when Jesus speaks to her, she asks, "How is it that you, a Jew, ask for a drink from me, a woman of Samaria?" Remember also that the text of John 4 says that "he had to pass through Samaria" to reach this woman. Jews of the day would go out of their way so that they did not have to go through Samaria because there was such animosity toward Samaritans.

So it is significant that the Gospel goes to Samaria, and it is significant that Peter and John verify that it has! Don't forget! The Gospel is supposed to go to Judea *and Samaria!*

> Now when the apostles at Jerusalem heard that Samaria had received the word of God, they sent to them Peter and John, who came down and prayed for them that they might receive the Holy Spirit, for he had not yet fallen on any of them, but they had only been baptized in the name of the Lord Jesus.

> Then they laid their hands on them and they received the Holy Spirit. (Acts 8:14–17 ESV)

This interesting passage is viewed by some as evidence for their position that baptism with the Spirit is an experience subsequent to conversion. They view this as *normative*. That is not my position. I believe it is *transitional.* I believe that baptism of the Spirit takes place at conversion and that this is a unique circumstance because of the early church and the Holy Spirit's movement among them. As we see the gospel move from Jerusalem to Judea/Samaria, we see the Spirit moving among those who are converted. Peter must be involved because he has "the keys" (Matt. 16:19). And the Spirit must fall on them as He had in Jerusalem, so that there was no doubt that they too had been accepted into the community of believers so that it was clear to the Jewish Christians that the converted Samaritans were included among God's people.

Seeing this caused strong reaction by Simon the sorcerer. Clearly, we get to see *the man's proposition*. He appears to not necessarily have interest in receiving the Spirit himself, but in receiving the ability to lay hands on people and have the kind of results that Peter and John had. This would be great for business! He even offers money to the apostles! He wanted the power of God not necessarily the person of God!

> Now when Simon saw that the Spirit was given through the laying on of the apostles' hands, he offered them money, saying, "Give me this power also, so that anyone on whom I lay my hands may receive the Holy Spirit." (Acts 8:18–19 ESV)
>
> This attempt to buy the gift of God elicits a strong, strong response from Peter.
>
> But Peter said to him, "May your silver perish with you, because you thought you could obtain the gift of God with money!" (Acts 8:20–23 ESV)

> You have neither part nor lot in this matter, for your heart is not right before God.
>
> Repent, therefore, of this wickedness of yours, and pray to the Lord that, if possible, the intent of your heart may be forgiven you.
>
> For I see that you are in the gall of bitterness and in the bond of iniquity.

It is clear that Peter sees Simon as still being unregenerate and in that we see *the man's peril.* Notice how strong Peter's language is:

- "May your silver perish with you." That is strong language to use with a believer. Peter saw Simon's money perishing and him perishing with it!
- "You have neither part nor lot in this matter."
- "Your heart is not right before God."
- "Repent." "While it is not out of place for believers to repent (see Rev. 2–3), the command to repent is usually given to unbelievers."[95]
- "Intent." "The word…means 'plot or scheme' and is used in a bad sense."[96]
- "For I see (present tense) that you are (presently) in the gall of bitterness and in the bond of iniquity." To be in bondage to iniquity would "indicate that he had never truly been born again."[97]

Simon's belief was superficial and never genuine. Here are two writers who echo my thoughts that have been expressed in this chapter: "His faith was like that of the people of Jerusalem who witnessed our Lord's miracles (John 2:23–25), or even like that of the demons (James 2:19)."[98] "This is one place in the Bible where the meaning of 'believe' falls short of saving faith. Not all who profess faith in Christ are true believers."[99] "This episode only shows how close a person can come to salvation and still not be converted. Simon heard the Gospel, saw the miracles, gave a profession of faith in Christ, and was baptized; and yet he was never born again!"[100]

This story caused an axiom to develop for me: *Profession does not equal possession. Possession is evidenced by transformation!* That is what the New Testament says.

"Therefore, if anyone is in Christ, he is a new creation. The old has passed away; behold, the new has come" (2 Cor. 5:17 ESV).

This story in Peter's life points to a number of personal applications for our lives. One of them is to *be open to change*. In this story, the apostles move from "initiation to verification."[101] The Gospel is moving. The Spirit is empowering. What happens here is critical to maintain the unity of the early church. And remember, this is happening among the Samaritans! The apostles have to be open to change—the Samaritans are being invited in. They also have to be open to change regarding their roles as they come now as affirmers or verifiers.

Some have said that as we age, we get resistant, stubborn, or even mean. Someone else has said that we get *brittle!* You and I must be open to change as well. God help us to remain *pliable!* We must "keep in step with the Spirit" (Gal. 5:25)!

We also should *beware being motivated by what God will do for us and not by what God will do in us*! Simon wanted the gift not the giver of the gift. He wanted power, popularity, and probably the monetary means that would come with those things. We must check our "intent" and make sure that we want Him, not just stuff from Him.

During the time that I was working on this chapter, I attended a funeral of a young lady who died at forty-five years of age. Thirty-six hours before being shot by her boyfriend, a family member had told her of (if my memory is correct) twenty-three victim protection orders against this guy and asked if it was wise to be involved with him. Thirty-six hours later, he shot her in the face, and the bullet exited by her spine, leaving her paralyzed from the neck down for the rest of her life. A few weeks later, she took a turn for the worst and passed away. At her funeral, her sister, a godly lady who grew up in our Student Ministry, stood behind her sister's casket and sang, "Just give me Jesus." Is that the cry of your heart? It was not Simon's!

We should also *be alert to discernment.* Verse 23 says that Peter *perceived* (to be mentally or spiritually perceptive). We should ask the Lord to develop this in us and we should be careful to pay attention to what we discern. The New Testament often urges us in this direction.

> And try to discern what is pleasing to the Lord. (Eph. 5:10 ESV)

> And it is my prayer that your love may abound more and more, with knowledge and all discernment, so that you may approve what is excellent, and so be pure and blameless for the day of Christ. (Phil. 1:9–10 ESV)

> But solid food is for the mature, for those who have their powers of discernment trained by constant practice to distinguish good from evil. (Heb. 5:14 ESV)

Lastly, I want to suggest that this story urges us to *be careful regarding evil.*

"For your obedience is known to all, so that I rejoice over you, but I want you to be wise as to what is good and innocent as to what is evil" (Rom. 16:19 ESV).

We are to be "wise, skilled" regarding what is good and "innocent, pure" regarding what is evil. This may well be even more imperative in light of the day in which we are likely living.

> The Bible predicts that this phenomenon of wonder-working false messiahs will become more and more prominent as the end draws near (Matt. 24:24, 2 Thess. 2:9). This section of Acts therefore warns us that the presence of wonder-working power does not mean that the power wielded is God's power.[102]

> For false Christs and false prophets will arise and perform great signs and wonders, so as to lead astray, if possible, even the elect. (Matt. 24:24 ESV)

> The coming of the lawless one is by the activity of Satan with all power and false signs and wonders. (2 Thess. 2:9 ESV)

Watch out for the Simon's of our day!

20

The Day of Exhilaration

Acts 9:32–43

Someone has said, "Life can be so *daily*." I agree. In fact, sometimes it can be very discouraging and difficult. We have seen Peter in jail. We have seen him threatened. We have seen him struggle. We have seen him fail. They could be called *days of exasperation*.

I thank God that in *an adventure with Jesus* there are also *days of exhilaration*! They are days of victory. They are days when we get to be a part of what God is doing. They are days where you just have to say—wow!

Last fall, I read about someone who has experienced both *days of exasperation and days of exhilaration*. His name is Keith Wheeler.

> Keith is a missionary, but he would probably call himself just a follower of Jesus Christ. Since 1985, he has carried a 12-foot, 90-pound cross across 120 countries. As he walks, God brings people to him from all races and nations to have conversations about the cross. After many of these conversations, people walk away with a new-found relationship with Jesus.

Keith is a humble man who gives God the glory for everything he has done. He could tell you the story of the time he woke up in the jungle of Panama surrounded by Columbian guerillas, who all had their guns trained on him. As the standoff grew more intense, the guerillas began shielding their faces and yelling, 'La luz, las luz!' ('The light! The light!') They soon dropped their guns and ran off. God had shown up behind Keith, and His glory blinded the rebels.

As Keith has carried the cross, he has been run over, left for dead, stabbed, jailed and put in front of a firing squad. Once, he was speaking from a balcony in Jamaica when it gave way underneath him. He broke his leg in twenty-one places, and doctors told him he wouldn't walk again. But they didn't know the God who had called Keith to take up his cross and follow Him.

Since his journey started, Keith has walked across every war zone. From Rwanda to Nicaragua to Iraq, he has walked between the two warring factions, letting them know the Prince of Peace wants to do a work there…on October 25, (2018), Keith asked his friends to join him as he carried the cross from the praying hands at Oral Roberts University, up to the flame on the campus where he started this journey more than thirty years ago. When he completed this walk, he had carried the cross 24,901 miles, which is equal to the distance of walking round the world at the equator.

In typical Keith Wheeler fashion, when someone asked what it was like to finish carrying the cross around the world, he said, "I am not finished. This is just the first lap."[103]

In this text, we get to look at two *days of exhilaration* in Peter's adventure with Jesus. An interesting question to me is why does Luke chose to record these two specific events out of all the likely healings performed through Peter's ministry? I want to suggest that the reason may well be found in these two passages of Scripture:

> "Truly, truly, I say to you, whoever believes in me will also do the works that I do; and greater works than these will he do, because I am going to the Father." (John 14:12 ESV)

> Even the Spirit of truth, whom the world cannot receive, because it neither sees him nor knows him. You know him, for he dwells with you and will be in you. (John 14:17 ESV)

Please note the phrases: *do the works that I do; and greater works than these;* because *I am going to the Father*. This is an amazing promise by Jesus that it is because of His ascension back to the Father. That ascension would allow for the sending and indwelling of the Holy Spirit and the intercessional ministry of the Lord Jesus. Those two things would enable mere men to do the works that Jesus did and, dare we believe it, even *greater works*! Let's look at these two events through that lens.

First, we see *the paralyzed man*. His name was Aeneas.

"Now as Peter went here and there among them all, he came down also to the saints who lived at Lydda" (Acts 9:32–34 ESV).

There he found a man named Aeneas, bedridden for eight years, who was paralyzed.

And Peter said to him, "Aeneas, Jesus Christ heals you; rise and make your bed." And immediately he rose.

This passage presents Peter in the midst of pastoral ministry, going "here and there among them all" and it was a growing thriving church (see 9:31). We are not told if Aeneas was a believer, but to me, it seems extremely likely in light of the language used here including Luke's reference to the saints (*agois,* lit., "holy person"). This was one of Paul's favorite words but not Luke's. In fact, the word only appears four times in the book of Acts and three of them are in this chapter (9:13, 32, 41).

We are told that he had been homebound *for eight years* because of his paralysis. Peter invokes the name of Jesus and two miracles occur. The first is that *a man made his bed* (I can hear every lady say "Amen!")! The second is that a previously paralyzed man rose!

Back to the lens we talked about—it is interesting that Jesus healed a paralyzed man. It is recorded by this same author in Luke 5:17–26 (see also Matthew 9:1–8, Mark 2:1–12). This man was carried to Jesus by four friends who lowered him to Jesus through the roof! Jesus initially forgives his sins and then evidences His power to do so by healing his paralysis. Now, Jesus' followers are doing the same work that He had done!

Next, we see *the prominent woman.* Her name was Dorcas or Tabitha.

"Now there was in Joppa a disciple named Tabitha, which, translated, means Dorcas. She was full of good works and acts of charity" (Acts 9:36–41 ESV).

In those days, she became ill and died, and when they had washed her, they laid her in an upper room.

Since Lydda was near Joppa, the disciples, hearing that Peter was there, sent two men to him, urging him, "Please come to us without delay."

So Peter rose and went with them. And when he arrived, they took him to the upper room. All the widows stood beside him weeping and showing tunics and other garments that Dorcas made while she was with them.

But Peter put them all outside, and knelt down and prayed; and turning to the body he said, "Tabitha, arise." And she opened her eyes, and when she saw Peter, she sat up.

And he gave her his hand and raised her up. Then, calling the saints and widows, he presented her alive.

Peter has now moved about ten miles away from Lydda to Joppa, which is the modern city of Jaffa. It is a city with quite a biblical history because it is the place from which the Prophet Jonah embarked when he tried to flee from God (Jonah 1:1–3). I love Warren Wiersbe's comments regarding the contrast here:

> Jonah went to Joppa to avoid going to the Gentiles, but Peter in Joppa received his call to go to the Gentiles! Because Jonah disobeyed God, the Lord sent a storm that caused the Gentile sailors to fear. Because Peter obeyed the Lord, God sent the 'wind of the Spirit' to the Gentiles and they experienced great joy and peace. What a contrast.[104]

Tabitha appears to have been a model for all Christians who had been extremely active in her service of those in need. In fact, as he arrived, we see this amazing scene of widows weeping and showing things that Tabitha had made for them. This is a memorial service! They are celebrating her life. They don't appear to expect anything else.

Back to our lens—there is one recorded instance of Jesus raising a female from the dead, and it is the daughter of Jairus (Luke 8:41–41, 45–55). Peter had been there when that happened, and it is interesting how many of Jesus' actions he seems to follow here. Jesus too had sent the mourners out (v. 40, cf. Mark 5:40). Fernando suggests that Peter probably spoke in Aramaic, and his words, probably "*Tabitha koum*" differed in only one letter to Jesus' words, "*Talitha koum.*" Jesus had taken the little girl by the hand before He spoke to her and Peter took Tabitha by the hand after she had come to life.

So as you can see, Peter was *doing the works that Jesus had done*, but notice how they had an even *greater result*! Here is the account after the healing of the paralyzed man by Jesus:

"And immediately he rose up before them and picked up what he had been lying on and went home, glorifying God" (Luke 5:25–26 ESV).

And amazement seized them all, and they glorified God and were filled with awe, saying, "We have seen extraordinary things today."

Compare that to the account after the healing of the paralyzed man by Peter:

"And all the residents of Lydda and Sharon saw him, and they turned to the Lord" (Acts 9:35 ESV).

"All" is probably hyperbole here referring to a large number of people, but clearly it refers to an astounding result for the kingdom!

Here is the recorded result following Jesus healing Jairus's daughter:

"And her spirit returned, and she got up at once. And he directed that something should be given her to eat" (Luke 8:55–56 ESV).

And her parents were amazed, but he charged them to tell no one what had happened.

Now compare that to the recorded result of Peter raising Tabitha from the dead: "And it became known throughout all Joppa, and many believed in the Lord" (Acts 9:42 ESV).

Once again, there is an amazing kingdom result! I think that is why Luke recorded these two *days of exhilaration* in Peter's adventure with the Lord Jesus!

When I think of these truths from the perspective of Peter, they absolutely move me! I think he would tell us how amazing it was to know that God had chosen to use him! What a privilege! What a thrill!

I know this—from the moment Jesus saved me, it has been my great desire that He would somehow choose to use my life for Him. And when He does, it just amazes me! Looking back over my adventure with Him, I would say that in the early years it was probably exhilaration with a little bit of pride. Now I cry. Some recent examples are when I clearly sensed Him using my life and counsel in a pivotal moment with a couple preparing for marriage. I cried. They cried.

Or as I recently stood with a family in an ICU room thanking God for a man's life and for his imminent homegoing (which would happen before I reached the parking lot). I sensed His presence and that He was using my life for good in that family, at that moment. I cried.

Or during my own hospital stay as the Lord gave me the privilege of sharing Him with a nurse PA. I cried.

Or in a series of difficult meetings with a family on the verge of shattering, but the Lord chose to meet with us and use my life as a part of that to help that family toward healing and a bright future. I cried.

Or in my ministry responsibilities, He has recently chosen to clearly lead me in such a way that I have been able to give vision and the right leadership for this moment in our church's history. It has caused me to cry that He would be so kind as to lead in such a clear way.

It causes me to conclude this chapter with this appeal: *In our adventure with Jesus, let us cry out to God that He might use us!* Those will be days of exhilaration! I like the way that B. B. McKinney put it in 1937: [105]

> Spirit of the living God, fall fresh on me;
> Spirit of the living God, fall fresh on me.
> Break me, melt me, mold me, fill me.
> Spirit of the living God, fall fresh on me.

Or in a more recent day, the way that Matthew West put it in his song "The Motions": [106] "I don't want to go through the motions. I don't want to go one more day, without your all-consuming passion inside of me. I don't want to spend my whole life asking what if I had given everything instead of going through the motions."

It was the lyrics of this song that moved the life of a young man from my hometown, McAlester, Oklahoma. His name was Ryan McAfee. He was eighteen years old when he posted the lyrics of this song to his Facebook page, saying he wanted to live his life with a passion for God that the song talks about and inviting his friends to keep him accountable. It was one of his final postings before he died on March 2, 2009, in an accident when his car hit a load that had fallen from a tractor-trailer rig on US 270 near Stuart, Oklahoma.

His desire was even fulfilled in his death. Over two thousand people were in attendance for his funeral. The song was played and those in attendance were moved by his passion and more than a dozen people trusted His Jesus for eternal salvation.

Oh, that our heart would be—Jesus, use me!

21

The Day That God Expanded My Perspective

Acts 10:1–48

Isn't it something when God uses something or someone to change or heighten our perspective? It happened in early 2019 in Boston during the performance of some of the best classical musicians in the country known as the Handel and Haydn Society. But the memorable and perspective changing moment didn't come from anyone on stage at Symphony Hall. It came from the audience, right at the very end of Mozart's Masonic Funeral Music.

Someone yelled, "Wow!" and it resonated—not just in the hall but throughout the classical music community. It was just such a departure from typical audience protocol, which is why the president of the Handel and Haydn Society was absolutely thrilled.

"I was like, 'That's fantastic,' said David Snead. 'There's a sense of wonder in that "wow."' You could really hear on the tape he was like, 'This was amazing.'"

David was so smitten by the outburst, as was the audience, that he decided to try to find the voice responsible. "Who was that? Because he really touched my life in a way that I'll never forget," David said.

He decided to write to everyone in the audience. Eventually, that email found its way to concertgoer Stephen Mattin, who was there with his nine-year-old grandson, Ronan. Ronan is the one who shouted "wow," which surprised Stephen more than anyone.

"He just doesn't do that. You know, usually he's in a world by himself," Stephen said.

Ronan is autistic and considered nonverbal. But music has always been a wormhole into his heart and mind. As a thank you, David arranged for a private cello performance for Ronan. But Ronan's family said all thanks should go to David and the Handel and Haydn musicians who made that moment possible.

They said just hearing Ronan's reaction after being told for years he might never engage—what more can you say but "thank you" and "wow."[107] Through one "wow" everyone's perspective changed!

It is a moment like that which we encounter now in Peter's adventure. This next episode in Peter's life is clearly important to Luke the writer. It is a part of the longest single narrative in Acts (10:1–11:18—sixty-six verses). "The centurion's vision is described four times (vv. 3–6, 22, 30–32; 11:13–14) and Peter's twice (vv. 9–16; 11:4–10), and Peter alludes to the events again at the Jerusalem Council (15:7–11)."[108]

This tenth chapter "is pivotal because it records the salvation of the Gentiles. We see Peter using 'the keys of the kingdom' for the third and last time. He had opened the door of faith for the Jews (Acts 2) and also for the Samaritans (Acts 8), and now he would be used of God to bring the Gentiles into the church."[109]

In our last episode of Peter's adventure, we left him *in Joppa*:

While he was in Joppa (and God was at work in his life), God was also at work in another life in Caesarea, which was a seaport on the Mediterranean coast that was rebuilt by Herod the Great and named after Caesar Augustus.

If you have ever been to Israel, chances are good that you flew into Tel Aviv. Joppa (modern Jaffa) is two and a half miles south. From Joppa to Caesarea is 39.2 miles north. This episode is exciting to me because everywhere we turn in it, we are reminded that *God is at work*!

We see that God is at work *in Cornelius's life* (vv. 1–8). As a centurion, Cornelius was in command of a hundred Roman soldiers.

Centurions are presented to us in a mostly positive way in the New Testament and Cornelius, in particular, is presented as a person of piety. Two characteristics point to this: he is a man of generosity to the needy and he is a man of regular prayer. In fact, we catch him praying at about three in the afternoon, which would have been one of the three traditional Jewish times of prayer. He was a very good man and a very religious man.

But he was a lost man!

> It is interesting to see how religious a person can be and still not be saved. The difference between Cornelius and many religious people today is this: he knew that his religious devotion was not sufficient to save him. Many religious people today are satisfied that their character and good works will get them to heaven, and they have no concept either of their own sin or of God's grace. In his prayer, Cornelius was asking God to show him the way of salvation (Acts 11:13–14).[110]

In a vision of an angel, Cornelius is told to send for Peter from Joppa and he obeys immediately. A good question is why Peter? Philip the evangelist was already there in Caesarea (8:40)! It is because Peter was the one who had been given the "keys."

We also see that God is at work *in Peter's life* (vv. 9–23). As we have noted, God is going to use Peter to unlock the door of the Gospel to the Gentiles. But to do so, He must first *expand Peter's perspective*. He begins that work in the house of a tanner! Remember, that is where we last left Peter: "And he stayed in Joppa for many days with one Simon, a tanner" (Acts 9:43 ESV).

Being a tanner "was a demeaning trade in Jewish eyes, for strictly speaking, tanners were ceremonially unclean since they handled dead animals. A tanner's shop had to be on the outskirts of town because of the bad odor that came from it. Simon's home was by the sea (see 10:6)."[111] So what we have here is the "Lord dealing with Peter's prejudices and directing him to open the door for Gentiles to respond to the gospel—the very thing that Jonah resisted in the same city (Jonah 1:3)."[112] It is fascinating that "the particular person whom God asked Peter to meet was a top official of the army of occupation in the hated capital of Palestine!"[113]

The trance that Peter experienced is interesting to me. The word is *ekstasis* (4–7), "a state of being in which consciousness is wholly or partially suspended." In the LXX, it is used of Adam in Genesis 2:21 and again of Abraham in Genesis 15:12.

In the vision, the entire animal world is symbolized, and Peter initially gives a categoric refusal to obey the one whom he calls "Lord"! This is such a perilous place to be in. As Dr. W. Graham Scroggie wrote, "You can say 'No,' and you can say 'Lord'; but you cannot say "No, Lord!""[114]

Notice that Luke says that Peter was "wondering about the meaning of the vision" (v. 17) and that he was "thinking about the vision" (v. 19). The word translated "thinking," which appears only here in the Bible, means "to think about something thoroughly and/or seriously." It is used to indicate intensity of thought. God is using the repetition and Peter's perspective on purity and impurity to prepare him to accept Cornelius's invitation to visit him.

We also see that God was at work *in the Church's life* (vv. 24–48). It is astounding that when Peter arrived, he discovered that Cornelius had gathered relatives and friends to hear the message of life! "He was a witness even before he became a Christian."[115] To this gathered audience, Peter preached the gospel (vv. 34–43), and as he did, *the Holy Spirit fell on all who heard the word* (v. 44), just as he had at Jerusalem and at Samaria. This amazed the circumcised believers that salvation and the gift of the Spirit had come *even on the Gentiles,* but the will of God in expanding the church to include the Gentiles was so evident that no one could refuse baptism to the new Gentile converts. The entire incident had changed the perspective of the church as well!

There seems to be at least four implications in the episode for us to carefully consider. The first is that *God will reach the responsive.* Cornelius is a good example that God gives *special revelation* of Himself to those who respond to *general revelation*. Although Cornelius was a generous and prayerful man (10:2), he was not a Christian (11:14) and these acts on his part did not merit salvation. I like the way that Warren Wiersbe says it: "The seeking Savior (Luke 19:10) will find the seeking sinner (Jer. 29:13). Wherever there is a searching heart, God responds."[116]

I love the story that Ajith Fernando recorded about a chief in Malaysia.

> One day in the early part of this century, a chief in Malaysia was repairing one of his wooden idols when he told his wife, "This is foolish. Here we are worshiping these wooden objects, but our hands are greater than they are. Surely there must be a higher Being, the god who created all of us. Let us worship him." So, for twenty-five years they went into their prayer room every day and prayed to "the unknown God." One day a Christian missionary came along and introduced the chief and his wife to the Bible and to Christ. When they heard the good news, they rejoiced and said, "This is the true God we have been seeking all these years. We now believe in him." This couple had responded to the light they received through creation (see Rom. 1:19–20) and began a search that resulted in their hearing and accepting the gospel.[117]

The second implication is that *God will change those who are changeable.* He desires to conform us into the image of His Son. This requires transforming our minds and how we think about things and also involves transforming our lives and how we live.

> Do not be conformed to this world, but be transformed by the renewal of your mind, that by testing you may discern what is the will of God,

> what is good and acceptable and perfect. (Rom. 12:2 ESV)

> And we all, with unveiled face, beholding the glory of the Lord, are being transformed into the same image from one degree of glory to another. For this comes from the Lord who is the Spirit. (2 Cor. 3:18 ESV)

He often uses a variety of circumstances, over time, to bring about change in our lives. A prayerful, open heart is fertile soil for the kind of changes He desires to make.

> In verses 17 and 19 Peter was grappling intensely regarding the meaning of the vision when the Holy Spirit spoke to him…a passion for obedience makes God's servants open to changes with which they may at first be uncomfortable. God found in Peter a person who was open to living with the uncomfortable.[118]

The third implication is that *God is unbiased, and His people should also be unbiased.*

> So Peter opened his mouth and said: "Truly I understand that God shows no partiality." (Acts 10:34 ESV)

> Whoever says he abides in him ought to walk in the same way in which he walked. (John 2:6 ESV)

In this part of Peter's adventure, the Lord is clearly breaking down bias in the life of His apostle and in the life of His church. Later the apostle Paul explained that the breaking of these barriers was a result of the death of Christ.

"But now in Christ Jesus you who once were far off have been brought near by the blood of Christ"

For he himself is our peace, who has made us both one and has broken down in his flesh the dividing wall of hostility by abolishing the law of commandments expressed in ordinances, that he might create in himself one new man in place of the two, so making peace, and might reconcile us both to God in one body through the cross, thereby killing the hostility. (Eph. 2:13–16 ESV)

We will never move past our biases unless we have an attitude of repentance. If we are not careful, our hearts can become stubborn and can close our minds and refuse to listen to God's promptings toward change.

That is *not* our guy Peter. Upon realizing that he had been wrong in his prejudices, he openly admitted it (10:28). Even in his preaching to the crowd, he publicly confessed what the Lord had taught him (10:34).

It seems to me that a great aid in removing bias from our lives would be to focus on what we have in common instead of our differences. As a Christ-follower, I know these truths: (1) God shows no partiality, (2) all people have incredible value because they are image bearers, and (3) Christ died for them as much as He died for me! I have relationship with Him because He valued me, not because I had some merit that others did not have!

Finally, *God is always at work*! This passage is a great reminder of this truth. Remember how Jesus said it: "But Jesus answered them, 'My Father is working until now, and I am working'" (John 5:17 ESV).

He was at work in Cornelius's life. He was at work in Peter's life. He was at work in the life of the church. He is at work in our lives as well!

I read another example of this while working on this episode. It was about the Maltose people. They are a mountain tribe in India that has had such a high mortality rate that they were expected to become extinct by 2025. They almost never bathe since they have little access to water. Consequently, the rest of society rejects them.

People will not go near them because of the smell they emit. *What would you do if the Lord called you to reach them*?

According to Ajith Fernando, the Lord did call, and they went. Here are his words:

> Missionaries from the Friends Missionary Prayer Band began a work among this tribe. They not only visited their villages, they even lived in their homes beside them.
>
> By 1996, about 34,000 of the 85,000 people in this tribe had become Christians, and with the consequent change in lifestyle, there has been a significant drop in the mortality rate. The missionaries have paid a great price to reap this harvest. Four of them have died of the diseases that have been killing the Maltose: malaria, tuberculosis, and kalaazar. One of them was the young son of Patrick Joshua, the leader of this mission. He had received his master's degree in social work and went to live among these people to help with their social reconstruction. After his death three other young people went in his place—a costly but precious harvest indeed.[119]

Our God is always at work!

The day God expanded my perspective.

22

The Day I Responded to Criticism

Acts 11:1–18

Ajith Fernando wrote, "Criticism is something any creative person who leads the church into new areas of obedience and ministry will face."[120]

But I think that the truth is that *anyone* who leads will face criticism! In this passage, Peter certainly does.

"So when Peter went up to Jerusalem, the circumcision party criticized him, saying, 'You went to uncircumcised men and ate with them'" (Acts 11:2–3 ESV).

The "circumcision party" is a group of Jewish believers in the church who wanted to require circumcision of all Gentile believers, held strongly to Jewish custom, were very legalistic, and as yet, did not understand the relationship between Law and grace and the new relationship between Jews and Gentiles in the church. In fairness to them, I like the comments of Warren Wiersbe when he wrote, "most Christians today understand these truths; but, after all, we have Romans, Galatians, Ephesians, and Hebrews! There were many converted priests in the church who would be zealous for the Law (Acts 6:7), and even the ordinary Jewish believer would have a difficult time making the transition (Acts 21:20)."[121] Their main criticism was that they went in to the house of uncircumcised men and ate with them.

It is instructive to observe Peter's response. Some would reject the church. Some would embark on personal ministry outside the church and its criticism. Not Peter. He did everything he could possibly do to gain their approval and support. He heard their criticism and endeavored to win their approval.

I can note at least four lessons we can learn from how he responded to their criticism. The first thing is that *when responding to criticism be precise.*

"But Peter began and explained it to them in order" (Acts 11:4 ESV).

The word *explain* (4–4) is "to set forth." The word *in order* or *precisely* (3–5) is "point by point, in order, successively."

It reminds me of an old television show when I was a kid called *Dragnet.* Sergeant Joe Friday was famous for saying, "Just the facts, ma'am. Just the facts."

That is what Peter is doing here. He is precisely giving them the facts. He wanted them to hear exactly what had transpired and what the Lord had done so that they would not only embrace, but be united in pursing the new direction that the Lord was taking His church.

Secondly, *when responding to criticism note the Lord's direction.* On three occasions Peter referenced that it was the Lord who was giving him direction for what he did.

> And I heard a voice saying to me, "Rise, Peter; kill and eat." (Acts 11:7 ESV)

> But the voice answered a second time from heaven, "What God has made clean, do not call common." (Acts 11:9 ESV)

> And behold, at that very moment three men arrived at the house in which we were, sent to me from Caesarea. And the Spirit told me to go with them, making no distinction. (Acts 11:11–12a ESV)

> The third thing that I observe here is that *when responding to criticism involve witnesses.*
>
> These six brothers also accompanied me, and we entered the man's house. (Acts 11:12b ESV)

The Old Testament had established a law regarding witnesses that the New Testament continued to embrace. Note these texts:

> A single witness shall not suffice against a person for any crime or for any wrong in connection with any offense that he has committed. Only on the evidence of two witnesses or of three witnesses shall a charge be established. (Deut. 19:15 ESV)

> But if he does not listen, take one or two others along with you, that every charge may be established by the evidence of two or three witnesses. (Matt. 18:16 ESV)

> This is the third time I am coming to you. Every charge must be established by the evidence of two or three witnesses. (2 Cor. 13:1 ESV)

> Do not admit a charge against an elder except on the evidence of two or three witnesses. (1 Tim. 5:19 ESV)

The testimony of eyewitnesses was important. Peter was wise to involve these witnesses and since there were six of them, it was *double* the required amount!

Finally, *when responding to criticism utilize questions.* As Peter concluded his testimony in verse 15, he noted that the Holy Spirit came on them "as he had come on us at the beginning" or at Pentecost.

In verse 16, he revisited Jesus' promise of the baptism with the Holy Spirit. He is making a case for a Gentile Pentecost!

With this great evidence, he wisely asked a question, allowing them to draw a conclusion.

"If then God gave the same gift to them as he gave to us when we believed in the Lord Jesus Christ, who was I that I could stand in God's way?" (Acts 11:17 ESV).

You wonder if everyone involved held their breath awaiting the response that was to come. The response was amazing, and it brought glory to God.

"When they heard these things they fell silent. And they glorified God, saying, 'Then to the Gentiles also God has granted repentance that leads to life'" (Acts 11:18 ESV).

What we have here is a *move of God* that is being criticized by *the people of God*! It is being responded to by *the man of God* in an amazing way and the Lord uses it to resolve the criticism!

As we close this scene in Peter's adventure it is important to state, once again, that criticism comes with leadership, especially when that leadership involves change. Here are three interesting examples that I ran across:

- One of the most beloved pieces of music is George Frideric Handel's *Messiah*. "When it was performed for the first time in Dublin, Ireland, it was warmly received. But when he brought it to England, the reception was lukewarm."[122] The problem was that although the words were from Scripture, the style of music and the place it was performed (the concert hall) did not sit well with many.
- "William Carey attempted to place before a meeting of Baptist ministers the challenge of missions. He was rebuked by a senior minister with the words, "Sit down young man! When God chooses to convert the heathen, he will do it without your aid or mine."[123]
- "William Booth, founder of the Salvation Army, broke new ground for the church by going out to the poor, the alcoholics, and others considered undesirable in society. But

> respected and devout leaders of the church criticized him. Even the great evangelical politician the Earl of Shaftesbury, who was himself a champion of the rights of the poor, once announced that after much study he was convinced that the Salvation Army was clearly the Antichrist. Someone else even added that in his own studies, he learned that the 'number' of William Booth's name added up to 666"![124]

So let's be reminded that Peter was a part of a "God-thing" and yet, he got criticized for it! So if you lead, don't be surprised when you get criticized. Let this episode in Peter's life encourage you to consider carefully how you respond. Take pains to get your response right. Do the hard work of response so that the Lord has every opportunity to resolve things in such a way that it brings great glory to Him!

As I spoke about this part of Peter's adventure to the church that I pastor, I brought a man up in front of our church and asked him to help me put it in a visual way. I asked him to assume that I had just led regarding some aspect of our church in a way that he did not care for and for him to assume the posture of criticism. He immediately stuck out his finger and began to wag it in my face.

I noted that I had two choices at that point, I could cross my arms and, in essence, communicate that I did not care what he thought; or I could take the position of the great apostle. So at that point, I faced him squarely and put my hands on his shoulders. Then, I took the index finger of one hand and repeatedly placed it in the open palm of the other saying that Peter explained his decision *point by point.*

I then pointed upward toward heaven as I communicated that Peter said that the Lord led him to this. I then pointed toward six imaginary *witnesses* as Peter called them to confirm the events. Then I took my Bible and said *the Lord said.* Finally, I turned back to my friend and held out my arms in a questioning fashion and asked, "*So what was I supposed to do*?"

God seemed to use that visual that day to embed Peter's response into the hearts of our people. It was a response that the Lord used in a mighty way in the first century to preserve the unity of the church!

23

The Day I Had a Prison Break

Acts 12:1–18

It happened again just recently in the life of our church. I recently buried a wonderful, godly lady who had fought a courageous battle with cancer for several years. During the same time period, another, wonderful, godly one of our ladies also contracted cancer. Her initial diagnosis was just as bleak. Both ladies were prayed for by hundreds of people, maybe thousands. The second lady recently went in for a scan after her latest round of chemo. Her cancer was gone! Two ladies, same church, same prayer support—one story ends in what some would call tragedy and the other ends in triumph!

I have experienced this dilemma in my own life. Over twenty years ago, I had a large pituitary brain tumor. I was very blessed that it was benign and was able to be removed by surgery. My life has forever been altered by the medications I have to take, but my result was basically very good. About ten or twelve years after my situation, a young lady that I knew had almost the same tumor and circumstances, except she was a young mother with a whole house full of children and, if I remember correctly, was pregnant when the diagnosis was made. I remember visiting her in the hospital prior to the surgery and attempting to encourage her with how my surgery had gone. Hers did not go as well. The tumor was removed, but something during surgery affected her personality and some motor skills.

Her life will forever be different as a result. Why did my situation come out better than hers?

As we follow Peter through these early days of the Church, we are observing a similar dichotomy of tragedy and triumph. Such is the case as we look into the prison cells of James and Peter. Two of the inner three!

The first thing I would note is *the restraint by the government.*

> About that time Herod the king laid violent hands on some who belonged to the church.
>
> He killed James the brother of John with the sword,
>
> and when he saw that it pleased the Jews, he proceeded to arrest Peter also. This was during the days of Unleavened Bread.
>
> And when he had seized him, he put him in prison, delivering him over to four squads of soldiers to guard him, intending after the Passover to bring him out to the people. (Acts 12:1–5a ESV)

So Peter was kept in prison…

The source of the persecution was King Herod (Agrippa I). He was an evil man from an evil family. He was the grandson of Herod the Great, who ordered children to be murdered. He was the nephew of Herod Antipas, who had John the Baptist beheaded.

Herod was despised by the Jews and knew it. He persecuted the church in an attempt to win favor with the Jewish people and appear loyal to the traditions of the fathers. "Now that the Gentiles were openly a part of the church, Herod's plan was even more agreeable to the nationalistic Jews who had no place for 'pagans.'"[125]

As a result, James becomes the first of the apostles to be martyred. Seeing that this pleased the Jews, Herod went after our guy Peter. Surely, if they were pleased that he killed James, they would be thrilled if he harmed Peter. Sixteen soldiers, four for each watch, kept guard over Peter. Of course, the reason is because the last time

Peter was arrested, he mysteriously (miraculously) got out of jail and Herod was doing everything he could to stop that from happening again!

Secondly, we note *the request by the church*. I wonder how often in the history of the church it has experienced the two little phrases used in verse 5, "So Peter was kept in prison…but earnest prayer for him was made to God by the church." It is, of course, a report of trouble in the lives of one of the saints and the church's ready response in prayer for God's intervention.

I love the description of how they prayed—*earnestly*! In the original it is the adverb *ektenos*, which is related to *ektenes*, a medical term describing the stretching of a muscle to its limits. I find it fascinating that *ektenos* is used in Luke 22:44 to describe Jesus' prayer in Gethsemane. "The church poured the maximum effort they were capable of into their prayers for Peter."[126]

This *request by the church* is the turning point in this story. Oh, the power of a praying church! I love how the Puritan preacher Thomas Watson put it, "The angel fetched Peter out of prison, but it was prayer that fetched the angel!"[127]

Next we see *the rescue by an angel*. This part of the story is very intriguing to me. I can't imagine sleeping, much less sleeping soundly, if I was chained between two soldiers and facing the possibility of execution the next day! Yet Peter was so sound asleep that the angel had to strike him to wake him!

What could have possibly given Peter such peace? I suspect that it could have been the knowledge that the people of God were praying for him. It was probably also the promises of God and a confidence in His Lordship. But I suspect that it also had something to do with the promise of Jesus that Peter would live to be an old man before his life would end with crucifixion (John 21:18–19). Herod couldn't kill him! So an angel was sent to rescue him, and Peter had an angelic escort out of prison and even went through the first *automatic* gate (v. 10)!

Finally, notice *the response of those affected*. There was certainly quite a variety of responses to this miraculous prison break! For instance, there is the response of *a servant girl*.

"When he realized this, he went to the house of Mary, the mother of John whose other name was Mark, where many were gathered together and were praying" (Acts 12:12–14 ESV).

And when he knocked at the door of the gateway, a servant girl named Rhoda came to answer.

Recognizing Peter's voice, in her joy she did not open the gate but ran in and reported that Peter was standing at the gate.

We have to admire Rhoda for her courage. The knock on the door could have been Herod's soldiers. It took great courage to open the door in the midst of the persecution that was occurring. And her response to Peter's voice is one of sheer delight. She is so overjoyed that she forgets to open the gate for him as she runs to tell the others!

There is also *the response of the praying church.*

"They said to her, 'You are out of your mind.' But she kept insisting that it was so, and they kept saying, 'It is his angel!'" (Acts 12:15–16 ESV).

But Peter continued knocking, and when they opened, they saw him and were amazed.

This whole scene is almost comical! We know that *many* had been praying (v. 12). They had been praying earnestly (v. 5). They had likely been praying for days, likely night and day, but they were surprisingly unready for the answer to their prayers. "The answer to their prayers is standing at the door, but they don't have faith enough to open the door and let him in. God could get Peter out of a prison, but Peter can't get himself into a prayer meeting!"[128]

I think the way to put this is: The church believed that God *could* free Peter, but it did not necessarily believe that He *would* free Peter. It troubles me how often this could characterize my prayer life as well! Warren Wiersbe said that "good theology plus unbelief often leads to fear and confusion."[129] I wonder how many times I have prayed for something fervently, with unbelief that God would ever do anything about it practically?!

There are also *the troubled soldiers.*

"Now when day came, there was no little disturbance among the soldiers over what had become of Peter" (Acts 12:18 ESV).

It was not good to lose a prisoner. It could mean the loss of life for failure to do one's duty for these soldiers. I'm sure it was *no little disturbance* as they tried to figure out what had happened and considered their potential fate! Things are stirred up among the soldiers!

Then there was *the response of an angry king.*

"And after Herod searched for him and did not find him, he examined the sentries and ordered that they should be put to death. Then he went down from Judea to Caesarea and spent time there" (Acts 12:19 ESV).

After a desperate (and fruitless) search for the missing prisoner, this vicious ruler examined the sentries and then ordered them executed. He just kills someone else!

Finally, there was *the response of a hidden Christ-follower.*

"But motioning to them with his hand to be silent, he described to them how the Lord had brought him out of the prison. And he said, 'Tell these things to James and to the brothers.' Then he departed and went to another place" (Acts 12:17 ESV).

The threat to Peter was still very real so he went into hiding. He must have hidden well—we still don't know where he went!

This day in Peter's adventure leads me to four words of application that seem to leap from the story. The first is that *God is sovereign.* The Bible makes it clear that sometimes there is miraculous deliverance and sometimes there is not (Hebrews 11 would be a great example of this). Peter is miraculously delivered (for the second time, see Acts 5:17ff), but James is not. Both were a part of the inner three. Both were faithful to Christ. Both were likely earnestly prayed for. Their outcomes were very different.

It is a great reminder that *there is only one King on the throne and He is to be trusted*! We must be faithful and obedient to Him regardless of the outcome. Hopefully my response and yours will mirror that of Shadrach, Meshach, and Abednego.

> Shadrach, Meshach, and Abednego answered and said to the king, "O Nebuchadnezzar, we have no need to answer you in this matter.

> If this be so, our God whom we serve is able to deliver us from the burning fiery furnace, and he will deliver us out of your hand, O king.
>
> But if not, be it known to you, O king, that we will not serve your gods or worship the golden image that you have set up." (Dan. 3:16–18 ESV)

The second word of application is that *God always has the last word*. We are reminded of that as we get a last look at the life of Herod. He seemed large and in charge in this prison incident, but clearly the Lord is in charge and holds him accountable. In this case, his end comes very quickly.

> Now Herod was angry with the people of Tyre and Sidon, and they came to him with one accord, and having persuaded Blastus, the king's chamberlain, they asked for peace, because their country depended on the king's country for food.
>
> On an appointed day Herod put on his royal robes, took his seat upon the throne, and delivered an oration to them.
>
> And the people were shouting, "The voice of a god, and not of a man!"
>
> Immediately an angel of the Lord struck him down, because he did not give God the glory, and he was eaten by worms and breathed his last. (Acts 12:20–23 ESV)

The third thing is that *God's kingdom advances*.

"But the word of God increased and multiplied" (Acts 12:24 ESV).

It always advances! James is killed here. Peter will be killed some twenty years later. But God's Word and His kingdom continue to advance and will continue to do so until it has been proclaimed to all nations (Matt. 24:14). Here a great man of God dies, but *nothing of God dies*!

A great illustration of this truth is expressed in the story of the deaths of the five missionaries to the Auca Indians in the jungles of Ecuador. At their deaths, some elements of the secular media criticized the entirety of missions and, from their opinion, the waste of the missionaries' young lives. But as the years have passed, it has become evident that a sovereign God won a mighty victory for the kingdom through their deaths!

Finally, *God's people should pray*. Although we cannot presume God's answer and we must always submit to God's will (Luke 22:42, 44), we must engage in prayer believing that "the prayer of a righteous man is powerful and effective" (James 5:16). I agree with the words of Ajith Fernando:

> *Through earnest prayer we can influence the course of history, for God powerfully answers such prayers.*[130]
>
> The English preacher Samuel Chadwick once said, "Intensity is a law of prayer…there are blessings of the kingdom that are only yielded to the violence of the vehement soul." He gives several examples of this type of earnest prayer from the Bible: "Abraham pleading for Sodom, Jacob wrestling in the stillness of the night, Moses standing in the breach, Hannah intoxicated with sorrow, David heartbroken with remorse and grief"…he went on to say…"the crying need of the church is her laziness after God."[131]

The day I had a prison break

24

The Day of the Watershed Moment

Acts 15:1–11

This incident in Peter's life is a *watershed moment.* In case you are unfamiliar with that language, here is a definition:

"A watershed moment is a point in time that marks an important, often historical change. The pertinent original usage of 'watershed' is to describe a ridge of land separating waters that then flow into two different bodies."

Some might call this a *defining moment.* You may or may not be a fan of the Men's NCAA Basketball Tournament (often called *March Madness*), but I enjoy it. A lot of years they show clips of previous incredible shots and moments from the years past while playing the song, "One Shining Moment." Often one of those clips is from 1983 and the improbable championship won by North Carolina State over Houston. The clip is of the final basket and then Coach Jim Valvano running around looking for someone to hug.

This team of unsung players was like a David beating multiple Goliaths on their way to, and in, the championship. What is interesting to me is how he had his team prepare for this defining moment. His first practice with them began with them cutting down the nets. They did it day after day. From his first day as coach he said, "I want to win a championship." And he believed that he would, so he had his team envision doing just that!

I love guys (and gals) who step into the big moments of life. I read about one just recently. On March 31, 2019, columnist Barry Tramel wrote about a seventy-six-year-old Madill, Oklahoma, lawyer named Dan Little. He is an ultramarathon runner who doesn't believe in fearing failure or, what he calls FOF.

For instance, he had started the Leadville Trail 108 times. The ultramarathon goes through the Colorado Rockies, with elevations ranging from 9,200 to 12,620. Started eight times and never finished.

Then he had his friend, Tishomingo attorney Dustin Rowe send him a *New York Times* story about a 7-7-7 marathon, telling him, "This is you. Do it for your grandchildren." Here is how Tramel puts the rest of the story:

> But a funny thing happened in mid-February from Antarctica to Miami and five continents in between. Little didn't fail. He completed all seven marathons. Phooey on failure. He became the oldest person, by nine years, to finish the World Marathon Challenge, which has been staged since 2014.
>
> Little averaged seven hours, three minutes and four seconds for each of the seven marathons.
>
> "Of course, you never want to fail," Little said. "So, I worked hard. But I did not expect that I could do 7-7-7."
>
> The group of 41 runners—16 of them women—developed a strong bond. Not all finished every race; some were reduced to half-marathons. But all started every race.
>
> "One for all and friends for life," Little said. "That's just how we feel.
>
> You know, it was grueling. It was a very, very intense, focused week. But we just really had a tremendous experience."
>
> ...the racing started in Antarctica, where the weather was above freezing at the start but

> minus-20 windchill by the time Little and the other slower runners finished.
>
> Their chartered jet then flew 5 ½ hours to Cape Town, South Africa, which was experiencing an historic heat wave. Temperatures got up to 103.
>
> From there, an 18-hour flight to Perth, Australia, where they ran at night, along a beautiful river.
>
> Then a 10-hour flight to Dubai of the United Arab Emirates, where running along the oceanfront at night again provided some relief from the heat.
>
> Next, a 10-hour flight to Madrid, where the Spanish course had unexpected cold and difficult hills.
>
> Then a 17-hour flight to Santiago, Chile, with a night race through a big park in the middle of the city. "Difficult," Little said, "but you could smell the barn by then."
>
> Finally, 15 hours to Miami, where the race started late, at 8 p.m., and he finished in the middle of the night.
>
> Seven marathons, seven days, seven continents, all without checking into a hotel. All the sleeping and all the eating was on the plane.[132]

All of that at seventy-six!

Well, Peter is not running a marathon, but it is a watershed, defining, shining moment here in Acts 15. How the church defines salvation is at stake. You can almost feel the tension as you examine these passages.

"But some men came down from Judea and were teaching the brothers, 'Unless you are circumcised according to the custom of Moses, you cannot be saved'" (Acts 15:1–2 ESV).

And after Paul and Barnabas had *no small dissension and debate* with them, Paul and Barnabas and some of the others were appointed to go up to Jerusalem to the apostles and the elders about this question.

"But some believers who belonged to the party of the Pharisees rose up and said, 'It is necessary to circumcise them and to order them to keep the law of Moses'" (Acts 15:5–7a ESV).

The apostles and the elders were gathered together to consider this matter.

And after there had been *much debate*, Peter stood up and said to them…

It is the language of argument, debate, controversy, and argument! Some were arguing that salvation was Jesus plus *nothing*. Some were arguing that salvation was Jesus plus the Mosaic Law (notice the words "cannot be saved"). This was indeed a watershed moment in the life of the early church. The very gospel is at stake!

It was at this moment that Peter "stood up"! It took such great courage! I think we learn much about how to stand up in moments like these from Peter.

One of the things I think we can learn is that *in watershed moments be sure of the will of God.*

"And after there had been much debate, Peter stood up and said to them, 'Brothers, you know that in the early days God made a choice among you, that by my mouth the Gentiles should hear the word of the gospel and believe'" (Acts 15:7 ESV).

This choice that Peter refers to "in the early days" was looking back about ten years! His point is that the whole thing was God's choice. It was the will of God. He knew that because of *the Word of God.* God had spoken to Peter by way of an angel and the voice of His Spirit (chapter 10). He also had remembered a word from the Lord Jesus (11:16).

He also knew it was the will of God because of *the witness of God.* God bore witness to this and Peter saw it! I love the word used here about God. It calls Him "the knower of hearts."

"And God, who knows the heart, bore witness to them, by giving them the Holy Spirit just as he did to us" (Acts 15:8–9 ESV).

And he made no distinction between us and them, having cleansed their hearts by faith.

The second thing I think we can learn from Peter is that *in watershed moments we should be careful to appeal to others.*

"Now, therefore, why are you putting God to the test by placing a yoke on the neck of the disciples that neither our fathers nor we have been able to bear?" (Acts 15:10 ESV).

Peter's appeal is that they were trying the patience of God and inviting His judgment by imposing conditions on believers over and above what God Himself had required. It is a wise and timely appeal. We, too, would be wise to give timely and well-reasoned appeals. We, too, should utilize questions with the word *why*.

This is a good opportunity to think through the conflicts that often happen among Christians and allow the implications of this text to guide us in our discussion and debate. The first thing I would suggest is that *genuine Christian character should be evidenced during discussion and debate.* Peter spoke "after there had been much debate" (v. 7). There is reason to believe that he listened and that he gave others time to express their position. It appears that he treated everyone with respect and gave value to their views even if he disagreed. It also appears that it was not personal. He valued what was best for the kingdom. He is more mature and grace-filled than the man we saw before the Resurrection.

The second thing I would say is that *Christian leaders should participate in debate with statesmanlike behavior.* I agree with Ajith Fernando who said, "Conflicts in the church today are often marred by a partisanship that reduces debate to the level of politicking."[133] I admire Peter and others here because they battled over issues not sides. They didn't favor a constituency. Peter, Paul, and James were Jewish! But they favored the truth and the whole of Christianity. It was not an us versus them battle! They were concerned about truth, about the kingdom and the glory of God—not about partisanship!

The last thing I would like to say is that, as Christ-followers, let's beware of what we consider a *watershed moment.* There are a number of things about which believers may disagree, but that they should not battle over. Here is a quick example. Every believer must believe that "in the beginning, God created the heavens and the earth" (Gen. 1:1). But genuine believers can disagree regarding when that beginning was. Some believe in a young earth. Some believe in an old earth. Obviously, someone is wrong and one day the Lord will straighten it out! The watershed issue is regarding the revealed truth about the designer.

But there are some moments, *watershed moments*, that are so critical and fundamental to the faith that we must respectfully say "no!" "I am willing to die for this!" In those *watershed moments we must be ready to stand regardless of the consequences*. This is one of those moments—salvation is by grace through faith—not of works. The error had to be confronted and there had to be a willingness to pay the price for salvation by grace through faith.

"No! We believe it is through the grace of our Lord Jesus that we are saved, just as they are" (Acts 15:11 NIV).

It is a great reminder that *Christianity is a religion of revelation*. Our God has spoken a definite and eternal Word to humanity. If a position opposes the revelation of God, we must say no! It is what Peter did here and what God's people have done throughout the ages.

- Joshua and Caleb said to the other spies, "No. God has promised. Let's take the land."
- Moses said no to the riches of Egypt and yes to disgrace for the sake of Christ.
- Joseph said no to the immorality of Mrs. Potiphar and yes to his God.
- Daniel said no to defilement and yes to vegetables and water!
- Shadrach, Meshach, and Abednego said no to false gods and yes to the fire.
- Paul (as we will see in our next chapter) will later say no to Peter and reaffirmed salvation by grace through faith alone.
- Martin Luther said no to Catholicism and yes to the book of Romans.
- Athanasius said no to Arianism, even if it meant that it was "Athansius against the world."

- Charles Haddon Spurgeon said no to "the boiling mud showers of modern heresy" and yes to the Word of God.

You may have a *watershed moment* around the corner in your life. If so, *be sure of the will of God*, *be careful to appeal to others* with the right kind of character and behavior, and *be ready to stand regardless of the consequences.*

25

The Day I Slipped

Galatians 2:11–14

I love stories of adventure and triumph in the human struggle! An example of that is an Australian named Cliff Young. He grew up on a family farm of approximately two thousand acres in size with approximately two thousand sheep. He was forced to round up the stock on foot when he was young, as the family was very poor during a time of depression and could not afford horses.

> In 1983, the 61-year-old potato farmer won the inaugural Westfield Sydney to Melbourne Ultramarathon, a distance of 875 kilometers (544 miles)… Young showed up to compete in overalls and work boots, without his dentures (later claiming they rattled when he ran). He ran at a slow, loping pace, and trailed the pack by a large margin at the end of the first day. While the other competitors stopped to sleep for six hours, however, Young kept running. He ran continuously for five days, taking the lead during the first night and eventually winning by ten hours. Before running the race, he had told the press that he had previously run for two or three days straight

> rounding up sheep in gumboots. He claimed afterwards that during the race, he imagined that he was running after sheep, trying to outrun a storm. The Westfield run took him five days, 15 hours and four minutes, almost two days faster than the previous record for any run. Between Sydney and Melbourne…upon being awarded the prize of $10,000 (equivalent to $27,200 in 2010), Young said he did not know that there was a prize, and that he felt bad accepting it as each of the other five runners who finished had worked as hard as he did—so he split the money equally between them, keeping none![134]

This story reminds me of Peter as we come to the end of our study of his adventure with Jesus! It is a wonderful adventure! And it ends with great triumph as far as I am concerned.

But first, it involved great tragedy. Since the resurrection of Christ, we have seen Peter mostly flourish. But in this episode, we see *the day he slipped* and slipped badly. I think that there are four things that Peter would say about this event.

The first thing I think he would say is *I was wrong*. That is certainly what Paul said!

"When Peter came to Antioch, I opposed him to his face, because he was clearly in the wrong" (Gal. 2:11 NIV).

This whole encounter occurred at Antioch and that seems significant. Remember that it was at Antioch that *the disciples were first called Christians* (see Acts 11:19–26). The believers were a called-out group of Jews and Gentiles

> whose identity and self-definition centered neither in their Jewishness nor their Gentile character, but rather in their common devotion to the one in whose name they shared a common meal. Thus, they were called *Christianoi*, 'the folks of Christ,' originally perhaps a term of deroga-

> tion that soon came to be owned with pride by believers everywhere because it was so evidently appropriate.[135]

It is interesting that in this place of harmony where Christianity is being so clearly lived out that one of the strongest confrontations of the Bible occurs.

Paul uses strong language here. *Opposed* is "to set against, resist, withstand." The word *wrong* is translated *condemned* by some translations. It is a rare word only used three times in the New Testament. It is the word *kataginosko*—and is literally "knowledge against."

Why such strong language? Some have argued that Peter is simply exercising Paul's own strategy.

> For though I am free from all, I have made myself a servant to all, that I might win more of them.
>
> To the Jews I became as a Jew, in order to win Jews. To those under the law I became as one under the law (though not being myself under the law) that I might win those under the law.
>
> To those outside the law I became as one outside the law (not being outside the law of God but under the law of Christ) that I might win those outside the law.
>
> To the weak I became weak, that I might win the weak. I have become all things to all people, that by all means I might save some.
>
> I do it all for the sake of the gospel, that I may share with them in its blessings. (1 Cor. 9:19–23 ESV)

Isn't that what Peter is doing? The answer is no. Paul was doing what he was doing among unbelievers in order that he might reach them. Peter is among believers and he is causing something that Paul saw as *sin* and as *out of step with the truth of the gospel.*

"But when I saw that their conduct was not in step with the truth of the gospel, I said to Cephas before them all, 'If you, though a Jew, live like a Gentile and not like a Jew, how can you force the Gentiles to live like Jews?'" (Gal. 2:14 ESV).

At least two things are true regarding how this was out of step. The first is that he was disrupting table fellowship among believers. Before this incident, Peter was sharing table fellowship with everyone. It was important. It was shared community. It communicated oneness in Christ. It communicated that the gospel was for everybody (see Galatians 3:28).

It is also out of step with the gospel because it is adding *works* of the law to faith in Christ.

> We ourselves are Jews by birth and not Gentile sinners; yet we know that a person is not justified by works of the law but through faith in Jesus Christ, so we also have believed in Christ Jesus, in order to be justified by faith in Christ and not by works of the law, because by works of the law no one will be justified. (Gal. 2:15–16 ESV)

This was not merely some personality clash between two apostles, but in Paul's mind, it was an attack on the very Gospel itself! The truth of the Gospel was at stake and the unity of the church was at stake! John Calvin said, "It is foolish to defend what the Holy Spirit has condemned by the mouth of Paul. This was no business matter but involved the purity of the gospel."[136]

I really like the way that Scot McKnight says it:

> The sharing of a common meal was a visible and socially powerful symbol of the new slogan Paul was teaching his young churches 'there is neither Jew nor Greek, slave nor free, male nor female, for you are all one in Christ Jesus'—

> Galatians 3:28…Peter was theologically wrong and dangerous.[137]

This was quite the slip for Peter. He was very wrong! It is often hard for people to admit being wrong. While working on this incident I watched a rerun of the old sitcom called *Tool Time*. In the episode, Jill and Tim had conflict between them. It ended with her telling him that he was right! He just couldn't leave it alone and said, "If I was right, that means that you were…?" The next few minutes of the episode were of her fashioning different responses, but never admitting that she was wrong!

As I said, it is often hard for people to admit being wrong, but I believe that Peter would definitely own up to being wrong at this place in his adventure with Jesus.

I also believe that he would say *I was a hypocrite.*

"For before certain men came from James, he was eating with the Gentiles; but when they came he drew back and separated himself, fearing the circumcision party" (Gal. 2:12–13 ESV).

And the rest of the Jews acted hypocritically along with him…

The words *acted hypocritically* are one word in the Greek text. It is only used here in the New Testament. It was a "theatrical term for the person who wore a mask on stage and who often interpreted the scene for the audience. In time, the term was used for the person who 'play acted' a role, this usage naturally leading to a moral description of someone who was insincere or fake (our term 'hypocrite')."[138] This is "the act of wearing a mask or playing a part in a drama. By negative transference it came to mean pretense, insincerity, acting in a fashion that belies one's true convictions… Peter had donned a mask of pretense; he was shamefully acting a part contrary to his own true convictions."[139]

It was pretense. A hypocrite is someone who says one thing, but they do another. Unfortunately, in this incident, it is Peter! Here was the apostle Peter who supposedly believed that salvation was by grace through faith alone and available to all. Yet he is living contrary to those truths!

I think Peter would also say *I was hurtful.* What Peter did not only affected him, it affected the church. It hurt others. Verse 13 says that others were led astray.

"And the rest of the Jews acted hypocritically along with him, so that even Barnabas was led astray by their hypocrisy" (Gal. 2:13 ESV).

There are two stunning words there…*even Barnabas*! One wonders the feelings in the heart of the apostle Paul when he wrote those words…*even Barnabas!*

Remember Barnabas? The son of encouragement. The guy that blessed the church everywhere he went. The guy who sought Paul out after his conversion and brought him into access and acceptance with the apostles. It was Barnabas who went with Paul on his first missionary journey. It was Barnabas who helped Paul with the work at Antioch.

What Peter did was so pervasive it affected *even Barnabas!*

"But when I saw that their conduct was not in step with the truth of the gospel, I said to Cephas before them all, 'If you, though a Jew, live like a Gentile and not like a Jew, how can you force the Gentiles to live like Jews?'" (Gal. 2:14 ESV).

The words "in step" are one word in the Greek. It is such a rare word that it is only used here in the New Testament. It is the word *orthopodeo.* We get our word orthopedics from it. It means "to walk straightly." It is negated by the word *not.* What Paul is saying is that Peter was *out of line* and his "out of line-ment" is affecting many others.

Lastly (triumphantly), I think Peter would say *I was helped*!

Paul's rebuke was not fun. It never is. But it can be so helpful if it is delivered in the right spirit and responded to with humility.

I know personally what this is like. Many have spoken into my life over the years and as a result I was helped. One of the finest examples for me was when a couple in my church spoke to me, hesitantly, about lingering among the Body after I preached. Three things helped me to hear them, and it did indeed help my ministry immensely. You might ask yourself these questions as you attempt to hear someone trying to help you.

- Do they love me?
- Do they love the kingdom?
- Is it important?

This couple loved me. I knew they loved the kingdom. It was important. They didn't want me to be viewed by our people as unconcerned, or uncaring. They genuinely wanted to help me and put themselves in an uncomfortable position out of love for me and for the kingdom.

I believe that Peter was also helped by this difficult rebuke. I like the way that Timothy George says it: "Peter had fallen before and repented before, and we may assume that a similar pattern of remorse and renewal followed Paul's stern rebuke…from all appearances Paul's one public rebuke of Peter was enough to eventually bring him around."[140]

As we close out this episode of Peter's adventure with Jesus, let me make a few statements of application for us all.

First, *we all make mistakes*. That includes me and you. It also includes great leaders. Great leaders can fall (and so can we all, 1 Cor. 10:12). Recently our church watched the film *Billy Graham: An Extraordinary Journey* and Franklin Graham talked about how his father made a mistake with President Truman when he shared some details about their meeting and also used it as a promotional opportunity. He said his father never did that again. We all make mistakes. Let's learn from them!

Secondly, *beware the pressure!*

Do not be deceived: "Bad company ruins good morals" (1 Cor. 15:33 ESV).

Peer pressure is a part of every life. Therefore, it is critical who we surround ourselves with and who we are influenced by! Peter finds himself in this place because he yielded to the unhealthy influence of the circumcision party.

Thirdly, I implore you to *be open to reproof.* We all have blind spots. We need others to speak into our lives. We should especially be open to reproof when we know that they love us and the kingdom and when it is truly important. Notice how often the Proverbs encourage us to hear reproof:

> Poverty and disgrace come to him who ignores instruction, but whoever heeds reproof is honored. (Prov. 13:18 ESV)

> A rebuke goes deeper into a man of understanding than a hundred blows into a fool. (Prov. 17:10 ESV)

> Better is open rebuke than hidden love. Faithful are the wounds of a friend; profuse are the kisses of an enemy. (Prov. 27:5–6 ESV)

Finally, *don't let the mistakes define you. Let them mature you!* I think there is great reason to see this incident maturing Peter in a way that causes us to admire him and to allow our last glimpse of him to be one of triumph. Here are two reasons that I think this.

Frankly, it is hard to determine when this encounter in Antioch took place. There are scholars I admire who say it was before the Jerusalem Council and there are scholars I admire who say it took place after the Jerusalem Council. One esteemed scholar seems to me to take both positions in the same commentary!

Which position one takes has real implications on how Peter is viewed here. I take the position that this happens *before* the Jerusalem Council. I do so based upon three passages (Acts 12:17, 15:24; Gal. 2:12). If I am correct, it causes us to cheer the Peter who made this mistake, but who matured from it and stands boldly at the Council in Jerusalem!

There is another reason to think that Peter matured from this. Look at his last words regarding Paul as an older man:

> Therefore, beloved, since you are waiting for these, be diligent to be found by him without spot or blemish, and at peace.
>
> And count the patience of our Lord as salvation, just as our beloved brother Paul also wrote to you according to the wisdom given him,
>
> as he does in all his letters when he speaks in them of these matters. There are some things in them that are hard to understand, which the ignorant and unstable twist to their own destruction, as they do the other Scriptures.
>
> You therefore, beloved, knowing this beforehand, take care that you are not carried away with the error of lawless people and lose your own stability.
>
> But grow in the grace and knowledge of our Lord and Savior Jesus Christ. To him be the glory both now and to the day of eternity. Amen. (2 Pet. 3:14–18 ESV)

Wow! He calls him *our beloved Paul*! What a way to characterize a man who, years ago, had publicly rebuked you! What maturity and growth! By the grace of God, may you and I respond the same! That's the man I want to be!

Conclusion

We leave Peter to die a death that is unrecorded in the New Testament, but that tradition says involved crucifixion upside down (foretold by Jesus, John 21:18–19).

One last thought as we conclude the story of *Peter: The Man Who Went on an Adventure with Jesus*. In essence, we have been examining Peter's story. We have been reading his journal, if you will. His story is much like ours. It is filled with ups and downs, success and failure, and highs and lows. His story has impacted ours because it was not only lived, but it was also recorded for generations to come.

Every person who responses affirmatively to Jesus' call to come and follow Him embarks on an adventure with Jesus. And your story is worth telling. It is worth passing on. I encourage you to consider journaling your adventure with Jesus. I don't care if it is in writing or oral storying. Pass it on!

NOTES

Chapter 1

1 John Walvoord, *The Bible Knowledge Commentary: An Exposition of the Scriptures: Volume 2*, 216.
2 Warren Wiersbe, *Be Compassionate*, 48.
3 John MacArthur, Jr., *The MacArthur Study Bible*, 1521.
4 R. H. Stein, *Luke: Volume 24*, 169.

Chapter 2

5 Wikipedia, www.theguardian.com.
6 Warren Wiersbe, *Be Loyal*, 123.
7 John MacArthur Jr., *Matthew: Volume 2*, 440.
8 John Walvoord, *The Bible Knowledge Commentary: Volume 2*, 54.

Chapter 3

9 David E. Garland, *The NIV Application Commentary: Mark*, 219.
10 Dwight D, Eisenhower quote.
11 William Barclay, *The Gospel of Mark*, 126.
12 Garland, *The NIV Application Commentary: Mark*, 227.
13 Garland, *Ibid*, 222.
14 Garland, *Ibid*, 222.

Chapter 4

15 General Omar Bradley, as quoted by Dennis Rainey, "The Art of Parenting," 93.
16 Craig Blomberg, *Matthew: Volume 22*, 251.
17 John MacArthur, Jr., *Matthew: Volume 3*, 22.

18 MacArthur, *Ibid*, 22.
19 MacAarthur, *Ibid*, 28.
20 W. A. Criswell, *The Criswell Study Bible*, 1133.
21 MacArthur, *Matthew: Volume 3*, 28.
22 J. F. Walvoord, *The Bible Knowledge Commentary: An Exposition of the Scriptures: Volume 2*, 57.
23 Blomberg, *Matthew: Volume 22*, 254.
24 Charles Swindoll, *Two Memorable Minutes*, 119–123.
25 Abraham Lincoln, *The Gettysburg Address.*

Chapter 5

26 John MacArthur, Jr., *The MacArthur Study Bible*, 1477.
27 W. A. Criswell, *The Criswell Study Bible*, 1170.
28 Warren Wiersbe, *Be Diligent*, 88.
29 James Brooks, *The New American Commentary: Mark*, 142.
30 Brooks, *Ibid*, 141.
31 Criswell, *The Criswell Study Bible*, 1205.
32 William Barclay, *The Gospel of Mark*, 211.
33 MacArthur, *The MacArthur Study Bible*, 1424.
34 David Garland, *The NIV Application Commentary: Mark*, 348–349.
35 Wiersbe, *Be Diligent*, 88.
36 Brooks, *The New American Commentary: Mark*, 141.

Chapter 6

37 Charles Swindoll, *Improving Your Serve*, 40–41.
38 John MacArthur, Jr., *Matthew: Volume 3*, 88.

Chapter 7

39 John MacArthur, Jr., *The MacArthur Study Bible*, 1426.
40 Craig Blomberg, *Matthew*, 282–283.
41 Blomberg, *Ibid*, 283.
42 MacArthur, *Matthew:Volume 3*, 147.
43 Blomberg, *Matthew*, 283.
44 Warren Wiersbe, *The Bible Exposition Commentary: Volume 1*, 67.

45 MacArthur, *Matthew: Volume 3*, 156.
46 Wikipedia.

Chapter 8

47 W. A. Criswell, *The Criswell Study Bible*, 1139.
48 Criswell, *Ibid*, 1222.
49 Criswell, *Ibid*, 1173.
50 John Wesley.
51 John Piper.

Chapter 9

52 J. D. Grassmick, *The Bible Exposition Commentary: Mark: Volume 2*, 158.
53 Grassmick, *Ibid*, 158–159.
54 Josh McDowell, *Undaunted.*
55 McDowell, *Ibid*, 157.
56 McDowell, *Ibid*, 158.
57 John MacArthur, Jr., *Matthew: Volume 3*, 281.

Chapter 10

58 California Podiatric Medical Association.
59 Sermon Central.
60 Sermon Central.

Chapter 12

61 R. Kent Huges, *Disciplines of a Godly Man*, 202–203.
62 Hughes, *Ibid*, 203–204.

Chapter 13

63 John MacArthur, Jr., *The MacArthur Study Bible*, 1626.
64 Warren Wiersbe, *The Bible Exposition Commentary: Volume 1*, 388.
65 G. L. Borchert, *The New American Commentary: John 12–21*, 295.
66 Alfred H. Ackley, *He Lives* (1933).

Chapter 14

[67] John MacArthur, Jr., *The MacArthur Study Bible*, 1628–1629.

Chapter 15

[68] *Webster's Dictionary*, "Definition of Leadership."

[69] Ryan Aber, *Daily Oklahoman*, Head Coach Sherry Coale quote.

[70] Adolf Hitler quote.

[71] W. A. Criswell, *The Criswell Study Bible*, 1277.

[72] Ajith Fernando, *The NIV Application Commentary: Acts*, 76, 80.

[73] Fernando, *Ibid*, 85.

[74] E.M Bounds, quoted by R. Kent Hughes, *Disciplines of a Godly Man*, 181.

[75] MacArthur, *The MacArthur Study Bible*, 1634.

[76] Fernando, *The NIV Application Commentary: Acts*, 79.

[77] Fernando, *Ibid*, 78.

Chapter 16

[78] Rachel del Guidice, The Daily Signal.com, November 13, 2018.

[79] Ajith Fernando, *The NIV Application Commentary: Acts*, 109.

Chapter 17

[80] Ajith Fernando, *The NIV Application Commentary: Acts*, 142.

[81] Fernando, *Ibid*, 146–147.

[82] John MacArthur, Jr., *Acts 1–12*, 135.

[83] MacArthur, *Ibid*, 133, 136–137.

[84] Chicken Soup for the Soul.

Chapter 18

[85] Ajith Fernando, *The NIV Application Commentary: Acts*, 198.

[86] Fernando, *Ibid*, 199.

[87] Fernando, *Ibid*, 196.

[88] Fernando, *Ibid*, 205.

[89] Warren Wiersbe, *The Bible Exposition Commentary: Volume 1*, 422.

Chapter 19

[90] Ajith Fernando, *The NIV Application Commentary: Acts*, 271.
[91] Fernando, *Ibid*, 271.
[92] John MacArthur, Jr., *The MacArthur Study Bible*, 1648.
[93] W. A. Criswell, *The Criswell Study Bible*, 1288.
[94] Fernando, *The NIV Application Commentary: Acts*, 272.
[95] Warren Wiersbe, *The Bible Exposition Commentary: Volume 1*, 436.
[96] Wiersbe, *Ibid.*
[97] Wiersbe, *Ibid.*
[98] Wiersbe, *Ibid*, 435.
[99] Fernando, *The NIV Application Commentary: Acts*, 272.
[100] Wiersbe, *The Bible Exposition Commentary: Volume 1*, 436.
[101] Fernando, *The NIV Application Commentary: Acts*, 272.
[102] Fernando, *Ibid*, 276.

Chapter 20

[103] Walker Moore, "Rite of Passage," article from the Baptist Messenger.
[104] Warren Wiersbe, *The Bible Exposition Commentary: Volume 1*, 443.
[105] B. B. McKinney song, "Spirit of the Living God" (1937).
[106] Matthew West song, "The Motions."

Chapter 21

[107] Steve Hartman, *On the Road* series, May 17, 2019.
[108] Ajith Fernando, *The NIV Application Commentary: Acts*, 317–318.
[109] Warren Wiersbe, *The Bible Exposition Commentary: Volume 1*, 444.
[110] Wiersbe, *Ibid*, 445.
[111] Fernando, *The NIV Application Commentary: Acts*, 311.
[112] Fernando, *Ibid*, 320.
[113] Fernando, *Ibid*, 325.
[114] Wiersbe, *The Bible Exposition Commentary: Volume 1*, 445.
[115] Wiersbe, *Ibid*, 446.

116 Wiersbe, *Ibid*, 446.
117 Fernando, *The NIV Application Commentary: Acts*, 342–343.
118 Fernando, *Ibid*, 324.
119 Fernando, *Ibid*, 331.

Chapter 22

120 Ajith Fernando, *The NIV Application Commentary: Acts*, 342.
121 Warren Wiersbe, *The Bible Exposition Commentary: Volume 1*, 447–448.
122 Fernando, *The NIV Application Commentary: Acts*, 254.
123 Fernando, *Ibid*, 257.
124 Fernando, *Ibid*, 257.

Chapter 23

125 Warren Wiersbe, *The Bible Exposition Commentary: Volume 1*, 452.
126 John MacArthur Jr., *Acts 1–12*, 322.
127 Thomas Watson quote.
128 Wiersbe, *The Bible Exposition Commentary: Volume 1*, 453–454.
129 Wiersbe, *Ibid*, 454.
130 Wiersbe, *Ibid*, 454.
131 Fernando, *The NIV Application Commentary: Acts*, 369.
132 Barry Tramel, *The Daily Oklahoman*.
133 Fernando, *The NIV Application Commentary: Acts*, 428.
134 Wikipedia.
135 Timothy George, *The New American Commentary: Galatians*, 172.
136 Timothy George, *Ibid*, 177.
137 Scot McKnight, *The NIV Application Commentary: Galatians*, 99–100.
138 MacKnight, *Ibid*, 105.
139 George, *The New American Commentary: Galatians*, 177.
140 George, *Ibid*, 81.

About the Author

Robby Roberson is a graduate of the Criswell College in Dallas, Texas (BA in biblical studies, 1992) and Liberty Baptist Theological Seminary (MA, 1995). He has been engaged in pastoral ministry for over forty years and has a passion for the Word of God and its proclamation. Robby is the lead pastor at Grace Place Baptist Church in Oklahoma City, Oklahoma, where he has served for the last twenty-nine years. He and his wife, Mellanie, have been married since 1977, and they have three children and six grandchildren.